THE KINGFISHER
ATLAS OF THE
MODERN
WORLD

Il...n

KINGFISHER

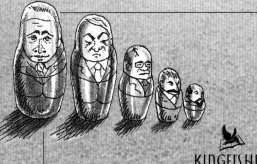

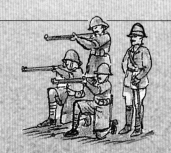

KINGFISHER

Kingfisher Publications Plc
New Penderel House
283–288 High Holborn
London WC1V 7HZ
www.kingfisherpub.com

Senior editors: Simon Holland, Selina Wood
Designers: Rebecca Painter, Tony Cutting, Mike Davis
Cover designer: Neil Cobourne
Consultant: Professor Jeremy Black, University of Exeter
Picture research manager: Cee Weston-Baker
Senior production controller: Jessamy Oldfield
DTP co-ordinator: Catherine Hibbert
Indexer: Clare Hibbert

Cartography by: Colin and Ian McCarthy
                Maidenhead Cartographic Services Limited,
                Maidenhead, Berkshire

First published by Kingfisher Publications Plc 2007
10 9 8 7 6 5 4 3 2 1

1TR/0607/SHENS/SCHOY(SCHOY)/128MA/C

ISBN: 978 0 7534 1375 3

Copyright © Kingfisher Publications Plc 2007

A CIP record for this book is available from the British Library.

Printed in Taiwan

CONTENTS

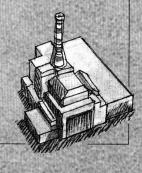

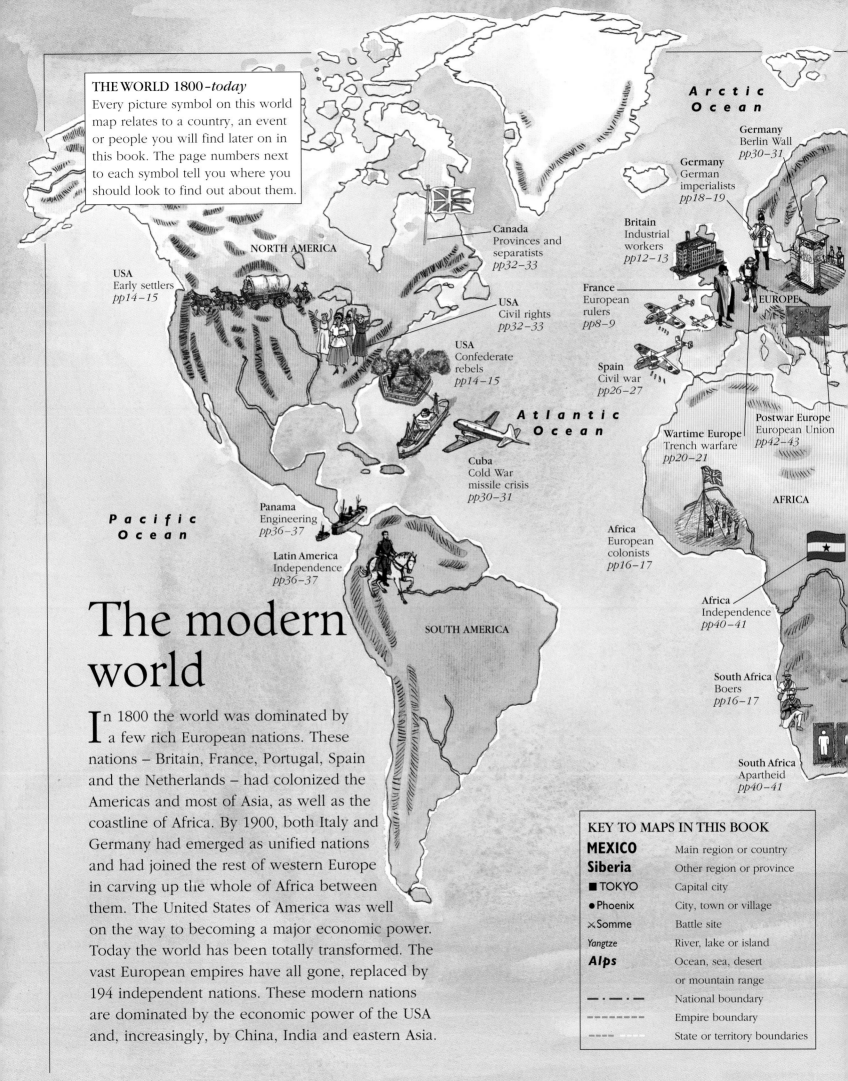

THE WORLD 1800-*today*
Every picture symbol on this world map relates to a country, an event or people you will find later on in this book. The page numbers next to each symbol tell you where you should look to find out about them.

Arctic Ocean

Germany
Berlin Wall
pp30–31

Germany
German imperialists
pp18–19

Britain
Industrial workers
pp12–13

Canada
Provinces and separatists
pp32–33

NORTH AMERICA

USA
Early settlers
pp14–15

France
European rulers
pp8–9

EUROPE

USA
Civil rights
pp32–33

Spain
Civil war
pp26–27

USA
Confederate rebels
pp14–15

Atlantic Ocean

Cuba
Cold War missile crisis
pp30–31

Wartime Europe
Trench warfare
pp20–21

Postwar Europe
European Union
pp42–43

AFRICA

Pacific Ocean

Panama
Engineering
pp36–37

Latin America
Independence
pp36–37

Africa
European colonists
pp16–17

SOUTH AMERICA

Africa
Independence
pp40–41

The modern world

I n 1800 the world was dominated by a few rich European nations. These nations – Britain, France, Portugal, Spain and the Netherlands – had colonized the Americas and most of Asia, as well as the coastline of Africa. By 1900, both Italy and Germany had emerged as unified nations and had joined the rest of western Europe in carving up the whole of Africa between them. The United States of America was well on the way to becoming a major economic power. Today the world has been totally transformed. The vast European empires have all gone, replaced by 194 independent nations. These modern nations are dominated by the economic power of the USA and, increasingly, by China, India and eastern Asia.

South Africa
Boers
pp16–17

South Africa
Apartheid
pp40–41

KEY TO MAPS IN THIS BOOK	
MEXICO	Main region or country
Siberia	Other region or province
■ TOKYO	Capital city
● Phoenix	City, town or village
✕ Somme	Battle site
Yangtze	River, lake or island
Alps	Ocean, sea, desert or mountain range
– · – · –	National boundary
– – – – –	Empire boundary
– – – – –	State or territory boundaries

Russia
Revolutionaries
pp22–23

Russia
Freed serfs
pp18–19

Russia
Space travel
pp22–23

ASIA

Middle East
Oil wealth
pp38–39

China
Communists
pp34–35

Japan
Kamikaze
pilots
pp28–29

India
Independence
pp40–41

Indian Ocean

Vietnam
Vietnam War
pp40–41

Pacific Ocean

AUSTRALIA

Australia
European
settlers
pp12–13

LOCATOR MAP
You will find a world map like this along with every map in the book. This allows you to see exactly which part of the world the main map is showing you.

POLITICAL MOVEMENTS
The following definitions may help you when reading this book:

CAPITALISM: An economic system based on private ownership, in which there is usually a free market to buy and sell goods.

COMMUNISM: A classless society in which private ownership has been abolished. The means of production and subsistence belong to the community as a whole, although this system is often under the control of the state.

FASCISM: An extreme political movement based on nationalism (loyalty to one's country) and authority, often military, which aims to unite a country's people into a disciplined force under an all-powerful leader or dictator.

FUNDAMENTALISM: A movement that favours a very strict interpretation of any one religion and its scriptures or laws.

MARXISM: A movement based on the ideas of the philosopher Karl Marx (1818–83), often known as the 'father of communism'.

NAZISM: A very extreme form of fascism, often involving highly racist policies.

1800
1800 Act of Union unites Britain and Ireland
1804 Napoleon crowns himself emperor of France
1807 Britain ends its involvement in the transatlantic slave trade
1815 Napoleon is defeated at Waterloo and sent into exile on St Helena
1821 Death of Napoleon
1825

1832 Greece gains independence from the Ottoman empire
1834 Slaves freed throughout the British empire
1839 Belgium gains independence from the Netherlands

1848–49 Gold rush in California, USA
1850

1859–70 Italy is unified as one nation
1861–65 US Civil War
1865 Slaves freed in the USA

1871 German empire created under Prussian leadership
1875
1877 Queen Victoria is proclaimed empress of India

1884–85 European nations agree to divide up Africa between them

1900
1905 Mass immigration to USA at its peak
1911 Chinese republic established
1914–18 World War I
1917 Revolution in Russia creates world's first communist state, which later becomes the USSR
1920 British empire at its greatest extent
1921 Ireland becomes an independent state
1922 Mussolini takes power in Italy
1924 Stalin takes power in Russia
1925
1929 Collapse of the New York Stock Exchange leads to worldwide economic depression
1933 Hitler takes power in Germany
1936–39 Spanish Civil War
1939–45 World War II
1947 India and Pakistan become independent of British rule
1948 Creation of the state of Israel
1949 Communists take over China
1950
1953 Death of Stalin
1957 Treaty of Rome sets up the European Economic Community (EEC), later the EU
1957 First artificial satellite sent into space
1957 Ghana becomes the first independent black African nation
1961–63 John F Kennedy is US president
1962 Cuban missile crisis
1969 US astronauts land on the Moon
1975
1979 Islamic revolution in Iran
1980 China begins massive economic expansion
1985 Gorbachev begins to reform the USSR
1989–90 Communism collapses across eastern Europe
1991 USSR collapses and is replaced by 15 new nations; the Cold War ends
1994 Apartheid (enforced separation of blacks and whites) is abolished in South Africa
2000
2001 9/11 (11 September) terrorist attacks in the USA
2002 Single, unified currency introduced in 12 European nations within the European Union (EU)
2007 EU now has 27 member states

2025

The world since 1800:
An endlessly changing world

The pace of change over the last 200 years has probably been greater than at any other time in human history. In 1800 the population of the world was about 930 million, and most of these people lived and worked on the land. Today the world is home to about 6.4 billion people, the vast majority of whom live and work in increasingly overcrowded towns and cities. New industrial techniques, mass communications and inventions such as the aeroplane and the computer have transformed the lives of almost everyone today, while few have been able to escape the effects of the wars and conflicts that have raged around the globe during the last century.

Industrial change

The Industrial Revolution began in Britain in the late 1700s, and spread throughout Europe and across to the United States during the 1800s. Millions of people who had previously worked on the land or in small workshops now lived and worked in large industrial towns. They laboured long hours in factories, iron and steel works and shipyards – as in New York (above) – where the working conditions were often difficult and dangerous.

Into space

The first artificial satellite to orbit the Earth, *Sputnik 1*, was launched in 1957. Twelve years later astronauts landed on the Moon, and by the end of the century they lived and worked in space for months at a time in orbiting space stations far above the Earth's surface (below). Unmanned spacecraft have now explored the furthest planets, sending back remarkable photographs of our solar system and beyond.

The impact of war

The 20th century was one of the most brutal periods in all of human history. Two major world wars and many other conflicts killed millions of people, and transformed the lives of many millions more. For example, women worked in jobs previously undertaken only by men, such as in heavy industrial plants (left). In many countries, women also gained the right to vote and to be treated as equals to men for the first time.

The International Space Station (ISS) is made up of separate modules, which have been launched into space individually since 1998.

Space Shuttle astronauts perform spacewalks to join the different modules together.

Communications

The development of the telegraph, postal services, mass printing techniques, the telephone, radio, television and the Internet have transformed communications over the last 200 years. This also means we have a huge volume of historical evidence to tell us about this period – photographs, printed material such as newspapers, and film and sound recordings. Today, information can be spread around the world in seconds via satellite technology, while computers are rapidly transforming the way we work, study, and entertain ourselves.

Television set from the 1960s

Early 20th-century telephone

Modern laptop computer

Newspapers are still an important source of up-to-date information. They are now printed and distributed at great speed, and in huge quantities, thanks to automated printing presses such as this one (above).

Mobile telephone with a digital camera

Napoleonic Europe

In 1804 Napoleon Bonaparte, ruler of France since 1799 and the most successful military leader of his time, crowned himself as Emperor Napoleon I. A series of brilliant victories then brought him control over most of Europe, with only Britain standing out against him. But in 1812 he invaded Russia in a final attempt to end its opposition to his rule. Although he seized the capital, Moscow, he was forced to retreat by the fierce Russian winter. Victories turned to defeats, and in 1815 a joint British and Prussian force finally overcame Napoleon at Waterloo.

After Napoleon

In 1815 the victorious European nations met in Vienna to agree the future shape of Europe. The old order of dictatorial monarchs was re-established, and few changes were made to national borders. Attempts in Spain and elsewhere to introduce limited democratic reforms were quickly crushed. In 1830, however, the people of Paris rose in revolt (above) against the dictatorial Charles X, setting up a new, more liberal monarchy.

these dotted lines show the borders between European countries in 1815

Battle of Trafalgar
The British navy under Lord Nelson won a victory against the French at Trafalgar in 1805, ending the threat of an invasion of Britain.

Industrial revolution
A revolution in the production of coal, iron, cotton and wool textiles turned Britain into the 'workshop of the world' by 1815.

Battle of Waterloo
Napoleon was finally defeated, at Waterloo in 1815, by the British and Prussians.

The Great Reform Act
The British parliament was reformed in 1832 to make it fairer and less corrupt.

Self-crowning
Napoleon became emperor of France in 1804, crowning himself at his coronation.

Sent far away
After his defeat at Waterloo, Napoleon was sent into exile on the southern Atlantic island of St Helena, 8,000km away.

Napoleon triumphant
In 1800 Napoleon crossed the Alps, soon to be master of Europe.

rural workers in the fields

The Peninsula War
The Spanish rose in revolt against Napoleon in 1808.

Temporary exile
In 1814 Napoleon was sent into exile by Britain and its allies to the island of Elba. He soon escaped back to France.

Fighting tyranny
In 1820 the Spanish army revolted against the brutal rule of King Ferdinand VII, but was crushed by the French in 1823.

French North Africa
In 1830 the French occupied the city of Algiers, the beginnings of a vast empire in North Africa.

Scotland

North Sea

Ireland

Dublin

BRITAIN

LONDON

Boulogne

Waterloo

Amiens

PARIS

Atlantic Ocean

DENMARK

NETHERLAND

GERMAN STATES

Rhine

FRANCE

Ulm

SWITZERLAND

ALP

Vitoria

PORTUGAL

MADRID

SPAIN

LISBON

Balearic Islands

Sardinia

Corsica

El

ALGIERS

Trafalgar

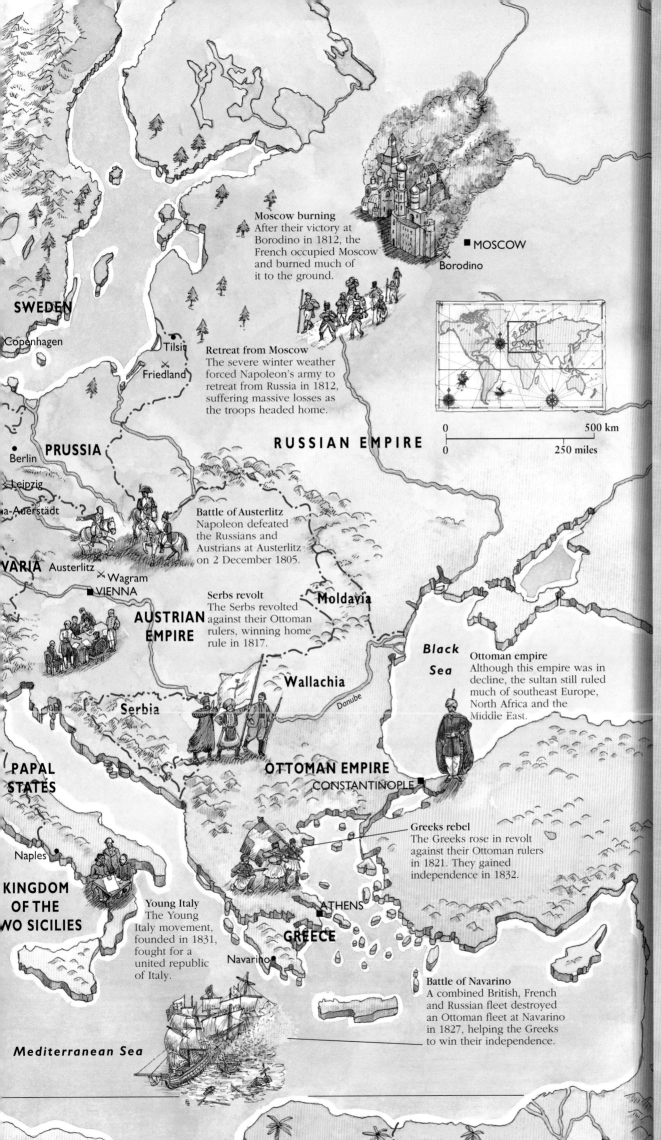

Moscow burning
After their victory at Borodino in 1812, the French occupied Moscow and burned much of it to the ground.

■ MOSCOW

Borodino

SWEDEN

Copenhagen

Tilsit

Friedland

Retreat from Moscow
The severe winter weather forced Napoleon's army to retreat from Russia in 1812, suffering massive losses as the troops headed home.

RUSSIAN EMPIRE

0   500 km
0   250 miles

PRUSSIA

Berlin

Leipzig

a-Auerstädt

Battle of Austerlitz
Napoleon defeated the Russians and Austrians at Austerlitz on 2 December 1805.

VARIA   Austerlitz   × Wagram
■ VIENNA

AUSTRIAN EMPIRE

Serbs revolt
The Serbs revolted against their Ottoman rulers, winning home rule in 1817.

Moldavia

Wallachia

Serbia

Danube

Black Sea

Ottoman empire
Although this empire was in decline, the sultan still ruled much of southeast Europe, North Africa and the Middle East.

PAPAL STATES

OTTOMAN EMPIRE
CONSTANTINOPLE ■

Greeks rebel
The Greeks rose in revolt against their Ottoman rulers in 1821. They gained independence in 1832.

Naples

KINGDOM OF THE WO SICILIES

Young Italy
The Young Italy movement, founded in 1831, fought for a united republic of Italy.

ATHENS ■

GREECE

Navarino

Battle of Navarino
A combined British, French and Russian fleet destroyed an Ottoman fleet at Navarino in 1827, helping the Greeks to win their independence.

Mediterranean Sea

1800

1802 Britain and France sign the peace treaty of Amiens
1803 Britain and France go to war again; Napoleon prepares to invade Britain
1804 Napoleon becomes emperor of Europe; he applies the 'Code Napoléon' (French civil law) across Europe
1805 Austrians and Russians are beaten at Austerlitz; British navy defeats French at Trafalgar, ending invasion threat

1807 Russians and Prussians are defeated at Friedland
1808 Peninsula War begins in Spain — a lengthy conflict fought by the Spanish and British against French occupation

1810

1812 Napoleon invades Russia, but the harsh winter forces him to retreat
1813 British under Wellington defeat French at Vitoria, Spain, ending Peninsula War; Napoleon defeated by Russians, Austrians and Prussians at the 'Battle of the Nations', Leipzig
1814 As enemies threaten Paris, Napoleon is forced to abdicate and is exiled to Elba
1815 Napoleon escapes from Elba, but is finally defeated at Waterloo and is sent into exile again
1815 Congress of Vienna redraws the maps of Europe and restores previous kingdoms: Norway is united with Sweden, and Belgium with the Netherlands

1820

1820 Revolutions crushed in Portugal and Naples
1820–23 Spanish revolt against Ferdinand VII ended by French
1821 Napoleon dies on St Helena in the southern Atlantic Ocean
1821 Greeks begin war of independence against Ottoman rule

1827 Anglo-French-Russian fleet defeats Ottoman-Egyptian fleet at Navarino

1829 Moldavia and Wallachia win home rule from Ottoman empire

1830

1830 Revolution in France: King Charles X is overthrown and replaced by Louis-Philippe
1830 French occupy Algiers
1830–31 Revolutions crushed in Italy and Poland
1830–39 Belgian revolt against Dutch rule leads to Belgian independence
1831 Young Italy movement founded
1832 Great Reform Act passed in Britain
1832 Greece becomes an independent monarchy

1840

Industrial Revolution:
Steam, iron and steel

The railways

The need to move raw materials to the factories, and to take away their finished products, led to a revolution in transport. A network of canals was built in Britain after the 1760s, but it was the invention of the railways in the early 1800s that led to the biggest changes. The first American steam railroad opened in 1830. Fifty years later there were more railroads in the USA (above) than in the whole of Europe.

An industrial revolution began in Britain during the 1760s. New machines, driven by steam and water, were used to manufacture textiles and other products in factories manned by hundreds of workers. Steam engines hauled coal and iron out of mines and powered railway engines to transport raw materials and finished goods. New technologies transformed the production of iron, steel and chemicals. The revolution transformed Britain – and later the rest of Europe and the USA – from a mainly rural society into an urban one. New industrial towns, where workers lived, were often squalid. Before long, people began to campaign for social and political reforms to improve living conditions.

Industrial towns

The development of factories led to the rapid growth of many towns, such as Leeds in northern England (shown below). Living conditions in these towns were often dreadful, as new houses for the workers were built back to back and close to the factories, mills and mines where they worked.

Smoke from factory chimneys darkened the sky and polluted the water supply

Nearby farms were quickly swamped by the expanding towns

Workers lived in cramped housing with few amenities

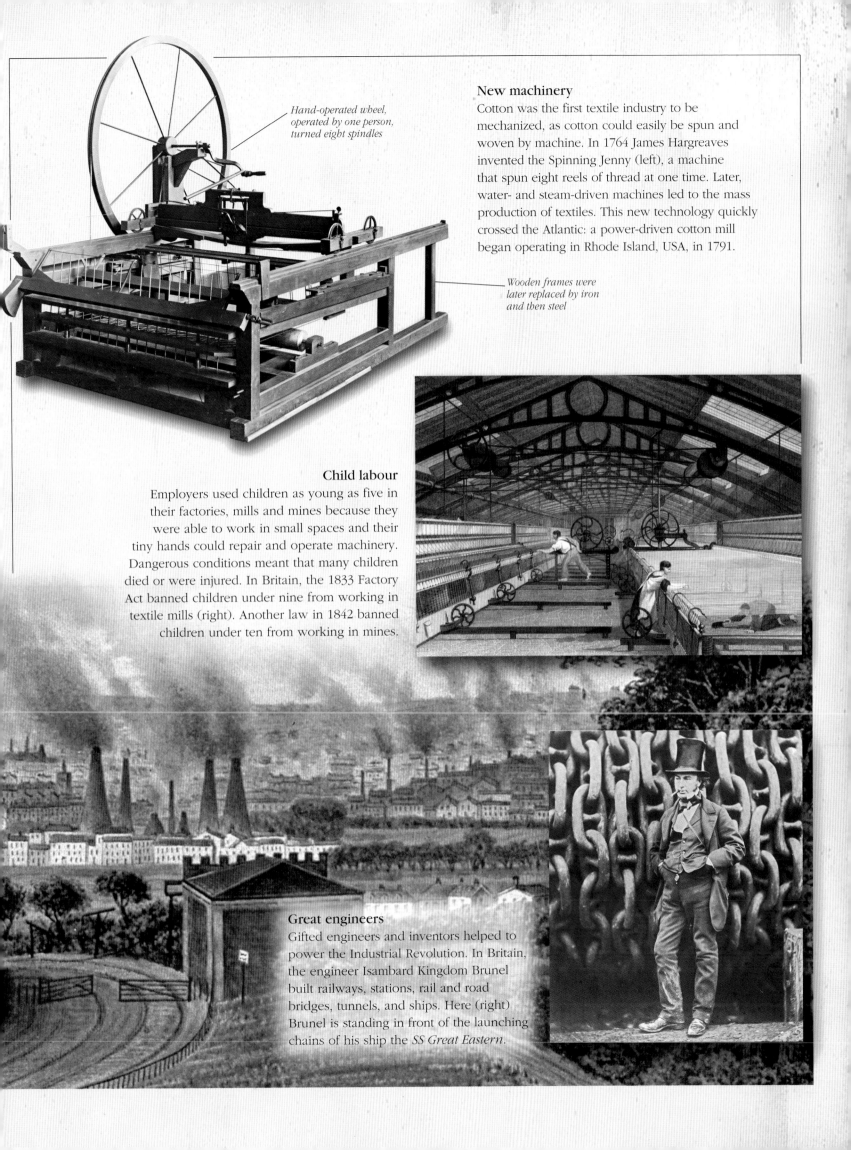

New machinery

Cotton was the first textile industry to be mechanized, as cotton could easily be spun and woven by machine. In 1764 James Hargreaves invented the Spinning Jenny (left), a machine that spun eight reels of thread at one time. Later, water- and steam-driven machines led to the mass production of textiles. This new technology quickly crossed the Atlantic: a power-driven cotton mill began operating in Rhode Island, USA, in 1791.

Hand-operated wheel, operated by one person, turned eight spindles

Wooden frames were later replaced by iron and then steel

Child labour

Employers used children as young as five in their factories, mills and mines because they were able to work in small spaces and their tiny hands could repair and operate machinery. Dangerous conditions meant that many children died or were injured. In Britain, the 1833 Factory Act banned children under nine from working in textile mills (right). Another law in 1842 banned children under ten from working in mines.

Great engineers

Gifted engineers and inventors helped to power the Industrial Revolution. In Britain, the engineer Isambard Kingdom Brunel built railways, stations, rail and road bridges, tunnels, and ships. Here (right) Brunel is standing in front of the launching chains of his ship the *SS Great Eastern*.

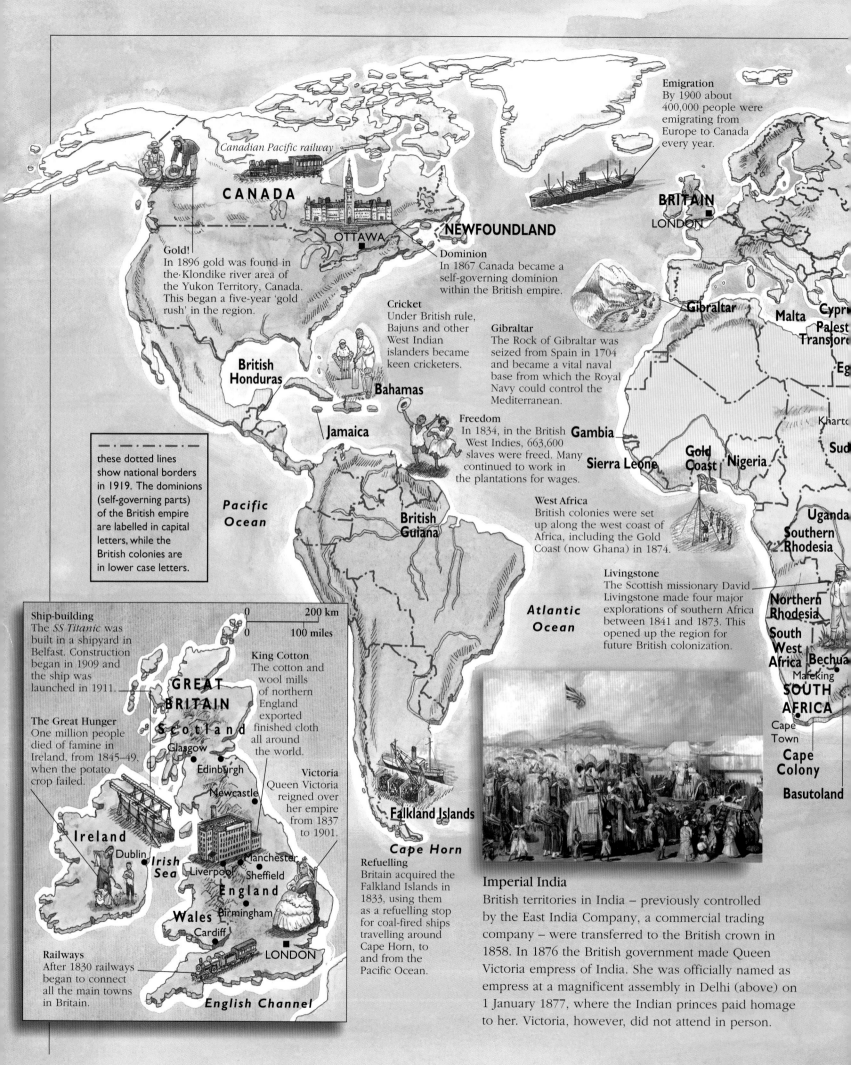

Canadian Pacific railway

CANADA

OTTAWA

Gold!
In 1896 gold was found in the Klondike river area of the Yukon Territory, Canada. This began a five-year 'gold rush' in the region.

NEWFOUNDLAND

Dominion
In 1867 Canada became a self-governing dominion within the British empire.

Cricket
Under British rule, Bajuns and other West Indian islanders became keen cricketers.

British Honduras

Bahamas

Jamaica

— — — — — —
these dotted lines show national borders in 1919. The dominions (self-governing parts) of the British empire are labelled in capital letters, while the British colonies are in lower case letters.

Pacific Ocean

British Guiana

Emigration
By 1900 about 400,000 people were emigrating from Europe to Canada every year.

BRITAIN
LONDON

Gibraltar
The Rock of Gibraltar was seized from Spain in 1704 and became a vital naval base from which the Royal Navy could control the Mediterranean.

Gibraltar

Malta

Cypr
Pales
Transfor

Eg

Freedom
In 1834, in the British West Indies, 663,600 slaves were freed. Many continued to work in the plantations for wages.

Gambia

Sierra Leone

Gold Coast

Nigeria

Khart

Sud

West Africa
British colonies were set up along the west coast of Africa, including the Gold Coast (now Ghana) in 1874.

Atlantic Ocean

Livingstone
The Scottish missionary David Livingstone made four major explorations of southern Africa between 1841 and 1873. This opened up the region for future British colonization.

Uganda
Southern Rhodesia

Northern Rhodesia

South West Africa

Bechua

Mafeking

SOUTH AFRICA

Cape Town

Cape Colony

Basutoland

Ship-building
The *SS Titanic* was built in a shipyard in Belfast. Construction began in 1909 and the ship was launched in 1911.

0   200 km
0   100 miles

GREAT BRITAIN

The Great Hunger
One million people died of famine in Ireland, from 1845–49, when the potato crop failed.

Scotland

Glasgow

Edinburgh

Newcastle

King Cotton
The cotton and wool mills of northern England exported finished cloth all around the world.

Victoria
Queen Victoria reigned over her empire from 1837 to 1901.

Ireland

Dublin

Irish Sea

Liverpool

Manchester

Sheffield

England

Birmingham

Wales

Cardiff

LONDON

Railways
After 1830 railways began to connect all the main towns in Britain.

English Channel

Falkland Islands

Cape Horn

Refuelling
Britain acquired the Falkland Islands in 1833, using them as a refuelling stop for coal-fired ships travelling around Cape Horn, to and from the Pacific Ocean.

Imperial India
British territories in India – previously controlled by the East India Company, a commercial trading company – were transferred to the British crown in 1858. In 1876 the British government made Queen Victoria empress of India. She was officially named as empress at a magnificent assembly in Delhi (above) on 1 January 1877, where the Indian princes paid homage to her. Victoria, however, did not attend in person.

The Suez Canal
Britain acquired 40 per cent of the Suez Canal shares from the khedive (ruler) of Egypt in 1875, giving it control of the waterway.

Protectorates
Britain gained a string of bases along the southern shore of the Gulf to help stamp out piracy and slavery in the region.

Afghan victories
In 1839–42 and 1878–80 the British fought two disastrous wars against the Afghans and failed to bring them under their control.

Mutiny!
A mutiny by the *seepoy* (native) armies in India almost ended British rule of the subcontinent in 1857.

Hong Kong
Britain acquired Hong Kong from the Chinese in 1841, and soon turned it into a major trading port and commercial centre.

Rubber
Rubber was first grown commercially in Malaya in 1896, with plants originally from South America and cultivated in England.

Iraq
Himalayas
Delhi
Lucknow
India
Bombay
railway at Bombay
Burma
Hong Kong
Kuwait
British gunboat
Oman
Aden
British Somaliland
tea growing in Ceylon

The Sudan
The British general Charles Gordon was killed when Islamic Madhist forces overran Khartoum in 1886.

Ceylon

Singapore
Britain founded Singapore in 1819. It soon became the major commercial port in the region.

Malay States
Singapore

Indian arrivals
During the mid- to late 19th century, Britain imported Indian labourers to work in the plantations of South Africa and build railroads in East Africa.

Gold strikers
In 1854 gold miners in Australia rose up to demand democratic rights in the mining areas, but they were defeated by British troops at Ballarat.

Pacific Ocean

North East New Guinea
Territory of Papua
Solomon Islands
New Hebrides (Britain and France)

Uluru

Indian Ocean

Cape Colony
The acquisition of the Cape Colony from the Netherlands in 1814 gave Britain control of shipping in and out of the Indian Ocean.

Anzac troops
Australia and New Zealand sent large numbers of troops to fight for Britain during World War I.

AUSTRALIA

Ballarat
Melbourne

NEW ZEALAND

Convicts
From 1788 to 1868 Britain shipped thousands of convicts out to Australia to serve their sentences in penal colonies.

Taking control
The British signed a treaty with the Maoris in 1840, which gave Britain control of New Zealand.

The British empire

Between 1800 and 1920, Britain carved out the biggest empire the world has ever seen. At its height, the empire covered about one-fifth of the globe – with colonies on every continent – and contained 410 million people, one-fifth of the world's population. The British built the empire to provide raw materials for their industries – such as cotton, silk, sugar, gold and diamonds – and a ready market for finished goods. It also defended vital British shipping and commercial interests around the world. Pride in British values, and a desire to convert local people to Christianity, were also reasons for its creation.

1800
1800 Britain gains Malta

1814 Britain gains Cape Colony from the Dutch

1819 Sir Stamford Raffles founds Singapore
1820

1830 World's first public railway opens between Liverpool and Manchester
1833 Britain gains the Falkland Islands
1834 Slaves freed throughout the British empire
1837 Victoria becomes queen
1839–42 Britain fails to subdue Afghanistan
1840
1840 Treaty of Waitangi between British and Maoris in New Zealand
1841 Britain acquires Hong Kong
1845–49 Great Hunger kills one million people in Ireland
1853–99 Britain establishes protectorates in the Gulf states
1854 Gold miners demand the vote in South Australia
1857–58 Mutiny breaks out in India
1858 East India Company dismantled; India transferred to British crown
1860
1861 Nigerian coast becomes a British colony

1867 Canada becomes a self-governing dominion
1868 Last convicts shipped to Australia

1874 Gold Coast becomes a British colony
1875 Britain gains control of the Suez Canal
1877 Victoria is proclaimed empress of India

1880
1882 Egypt becomes a British protectorate
1884 European nations begin to scramble for African colonies
1888 Britain gains Rhodesia (Zimbabwe)

1893 New Zealand women gain the vote
1894–95 Uganda and Kenya become British colonies
1896 Rubber first cultivated in Malaya

1899–1902 British crush the Boers in South Africa
1900
1901 Victoria dies; Edward VII becomes king
1901 Australian colonies unite to form the Commonwealth of Australia
1907 New Zealand becomes a dominion
1910 Union of South Africa created
1910 George V becomes king

1917–34 Newfoundland is a dominion

1919 Britain, Australia and New Zealand gain German colonies in Africa and Oceania
1920
1920 Britain gains Iraq, Jordan and Palestine – the empire is at its greatest extent
1922 Ireland becomes a Free State within the British empire
1922 Egypt becomes independent
1931 Statute of Westminster makes dominions independent and equal to Britain, and creates the British Commonwealth of Nations
1936 George VI becomes king after his brother, Edward VIII, abdicates
1939 Empire joins Britain in World War II against Germany, Italy and, in 1941, Japan
1940

The USA in the 19th century

In a little over 100 years, the United States of America transformed itself. It grew from a narrow strip of newly independent colonies along the Atlantic coast to a continental power that stretched out across the Pacific Ocean and up towards the Arctic. However, much of this new land was already occupied by native Americans, who fought fiercely to survive and keep their ancient heritage alive. By the end of the 19th century, the native Americans were confined to special reservations, and the USA was on its way to becoming the richest and most powerful nation in the world.

The American Civil War

The southern states of the USA allowed white citizens to keep black slaves to work on their cotton plantations and in their homes. Other states, however, were against slavery. The argument between the two sides erupted in 1861 when 11 southern states left the Union and set up the independent Confederacy. A vicious civil war broke out that lasted four years and killed at least 600,000 people. This picture shows Confederate fortifications near Petersburg, Virginia, in 1865. The Union, led by President Abraham Lincoln, eventually won the war and abolished slavery.

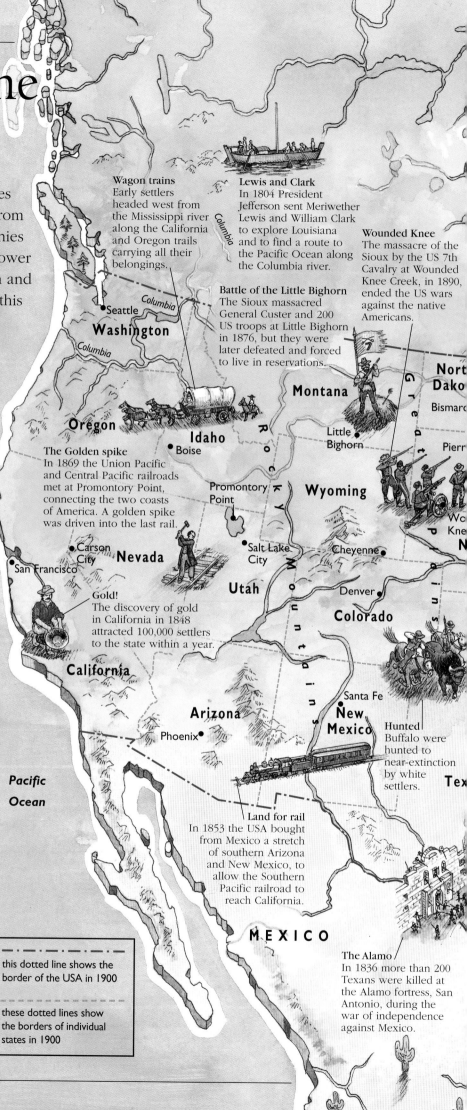

Wagon trains
Early settlers headed west from the Mississippi river along the California and Oregon trails carrying all their belongings.

Lewis and Clark
In 1804 President Jefferson sent Meriwether Lewis and William Clark to explore Louisiana and to find a route to the Pacific Ocean along the Columbia river.

Wounded Knee
The massacre of the Sioux by the US 7th Cavalry at Wounded Knee Creek, in 1890, ended the US wars against the native Americans.

Battle of the Little Bighorn
The Sioux massacred General Custer and 200 US troops at Little Bighorn in 1876, but they were later defeated and forced to live in reservations.

The Golden spike
In 1869 the Union Pacific and Central Pacific railroads met at Promontory Point, connecting the two coasts of America. A golden spike was driven into the last rail.

Gold!
The discovery of gold in California in 1848 attracted 100,000 settlers to the state within a year.

Hunted
Buffalo were hunted to near-extinction by white settlers.

Land for rail
In 1853 the USA bought from Mexico a stretch of southern Arizona and New Mexico, to allow the Southern Pacific railroad to reach California.

The Alamo
In 1836 more than 200 Texans were killed at the Alamo fortress, San Antonio, during the war of independence against Mexico.

Seattle, Washington, Columbia, Oregon, Idaho, Boise, Montana, Little Bighorn, North Dakota, Bismarck, Pierre, Wounded Knee, Promontory Point, Wyoming, Salt Lake City, Cheyenne, Carson City, Nevada, San Francisco, Utah, Denver, Colorado, California, Arizona, Phoenix, Santa Fe, New Mexico, Texas, MEXICO, Pacific Ocean, Rocky Mountains, Great Plains

this dotted line shows the border of the USA in 1900

these dotted lines show the borders of individual states in 1900

0   1000 km
0   500 miles

KEY TO EAST COAST STATES

1	Maine	7	Connecticut
2	Vermont	8	Pennsylvania
3	New Hampshire	9	New Jersey
4	New York	10	Delaware
5	Massachusetts	11	Maryland
6	Rhode Island	12	Virginia

CANADA

Skyscrapers
The Reliance Building, the world's first steel-frame skyscraper, was built in Chicago in 1895.

Model-T Ford
The first Model-T rolled off the Ford production line in 1908. Its low cost made car ownership possible for millions of people for the first time.

immigrants arriving in New York in the 1890s

Minnesota
St Paul
Wisconsin
farming on the plains
Iowa
Des Moine
Madison
Michigan
Lansing
Detroit
Chicago
Lake Superior
Lake Michigan
Lake Huron
Lake Ontario
Lake Erie
2
3
4
5
6
7
New York
8
9
Philadelphia
Gettysburg
10
11
WASHINGTON D.C.
West Virginia
12
Hampton Roads
Appomattox

Illinois
Springfield
Indiana
Indianapolis
Ohio
Columbus

incoln
Kansas City
Abilene
Topeka
ansas
Missouri
Jefferson City
slaves in southern plantations
ndian rritory
Oklahoma City
Little Rock
Arkansas
Kentucky
Tennessee
Nashville
Memphis

Burning the capital
In 1814 British troops burned down the White House during its war with the USA.

Surrender
The Civil War neared its end when Confederate commander Robert E Lee surrendered his army at Appomattox Court House, Virginia, in April 1865.

North Carolina
South Carolina
Charleston
Fort Sumter
Atlanta
Georgia
Alabama
Mississippi
Jackson
Louisiana
Baton Rouge
New Orleans
jazz musicians in New Orleans
Austin
Antonio
FLORIDA

Appalachian Mountains

Atlantic Ocean

Outbreak of war
The American Civil War began when southern Confederate troops bombarded Fort Sumter (a Union fort) in Charleston, South Carolina, in April 1861.

Oil wells
Oil was first discovered at Spindletop in Texas in 1901, giving birth to a massive oil industry.

Cattle driving
Cattle were driven north every year from Texas to Abilene for transport by rail to slaughter-houses in Kansas City and Chicago.

Forced removal
During the 1830s more than 100,000 native Americans were forced to move from the eastern USA to the Indian Territory (now Oklahoma) to make way for white settlers.

Gulf of Mexico

1800–1920

1800
1800 USA consists of just 16 states
1803 Louisiana purchased from France, doubling the size of the country
1804–06 Lewis and Clark explore Louisiana territory

1812–15 Anglo-American war caused by British attempts to prevent the USA trading with Napoleonic France

1819 Spain gives Florida to the USA
1820
1820 Missouri Compromise allows for equal numbers of slave states and free (anti-slavery) states to join the Union

1830 Indian Removal Act forces native Americans (then called Indians) to move to the Indian Territory

1836 Texas gains independence from Mexico

1840
1845 USA annexes (takes control of) the Republic of Texas
1846 Britain and the USA agree to divide Oregon
1846–48 USA goes to war with Mexico over its border with Texas
1848 USA gains California and other western states from Mexico
1848 Gold discovered in California

1853 USA buys southern New Mexico and Arizona from Mexico

1860
1860 South Carolina leaves the Union, followed by 10 more pro-slavery states
1861–65 Civil War between Union and Confederate states
1865 13th Amendment to the US Constitution formally abolishes slavery
1867 USA buys Alaska from Russia for $7.2 million and acquires Midway Island, its first Pacific island territory
1869 First Transcontinental railroad completed
1870 US population is now at 40 million

1876 Battle of the Little Bighorn
1880

1890 Sioux massacred at Wounded Knee Creek
1892 Ellis Island begins to admit immigrants
1895 First skyscraper built in Chicago

1898 Spain loses Puerto Rico, Guam and the Philippines to the USA
1898 USA gains Hawaiian islands in the Pacific Ocean
1899 USA acquires Samoa in the south Pacific
1900
1901 Oil found in Texas
1905 One million immigrants enter the USA each year

1908 First Model-T Ford car produced in Detroit

1910 US population is now at 92 million

1917 USA enters World War I

1920 USA consists of 48 states
1920

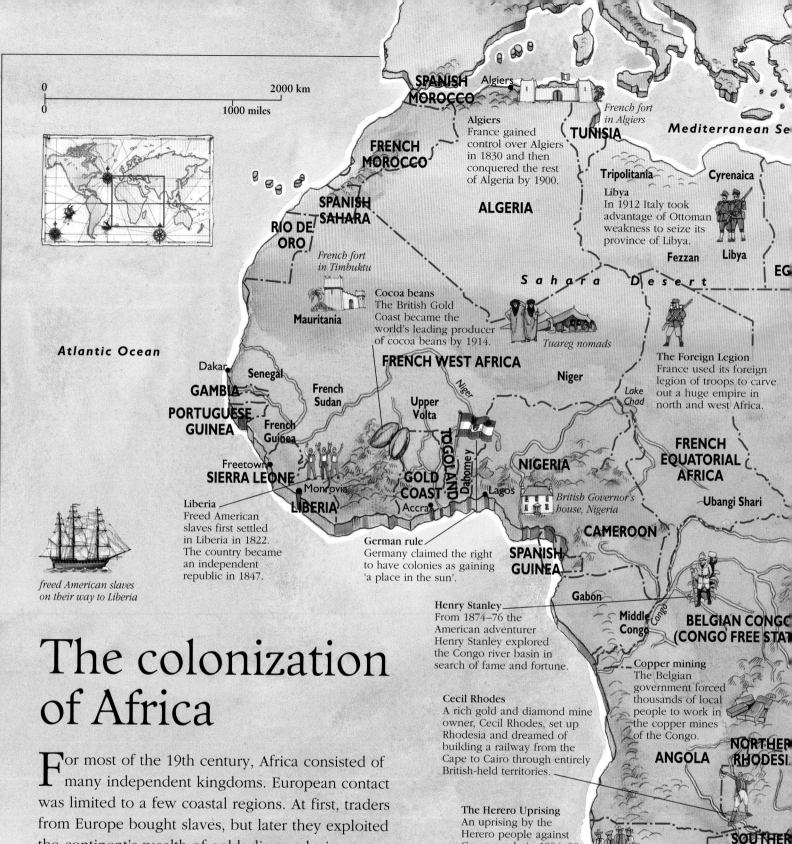

0 ——————— **2000 km**
0 ——————— **1000 miles**

Atlantic Ocean

Mediterranean Se

SPANISH MOROCCO Algiers

French fort in Algiers

FRENCH MOROCCO

Algiers
France gained control over Algiers in 1830 and then conquered the rest of Algeria by 1900.

TUNISIA

Tripolitania   Cyrenaica

Libya
In 1912 Italy took advantage of Ottoman weakness to seize its province of Libya.

ALGERIA

Fezzan   **Libya**

SPANISH SAHARA

RIO DE ORO

French fort in Timbuktu

Mauritania

Cocoa beans
The British Gold Coast became the world's leading producer of cocoa beans by 1914.

Sahara Desert

Tuareg nomads

FRENCH WEST AFRICA

The Foreign Legion
France used its foreign legion of troops to carve out a huge empire in north and west Africa.

Dakar   **Senegal**

GAMBIA

PORTUGUESE GUINEA

French Sudan

French Guinea

Upper Volta

Niger

Niger

Lake Chad

FRENCH EQUATORIAL AFRICA

Freetown
SIERRA LEONE

TOGOLAND

GOLD COAST

Dahomey

NIGERIA

Lagos

British Governor's house, Nigeria

Monrovia

LIBERIA

Accra

Ubangi Shari

Liberia
Freed American slaves first settled in Liberia in 1822. The country became an independent republic in 1847.

German rule
Germany claimed the right to have colonies as gaining 'a place in the sun'.

CAMEROON

SPANISH GUINEA

Gabon

Henry Stanley
From 1874–76 the American adventurer Henry Stanley explored the Congo river basin in search of fame and fortune.

Middle Congo

BELGIAN CONGO (CONGO FREE STAT

freed American slaves on their way to Liberia

Cecil Rhodes
A rich gold and diamond mine owner, Cecil Rhodes, set up Rhodesia and dreamed of building a railway from the Cape to Cairo through entirely British-held territories.

Copper mining
The Belgian government forced thousands of local people to work in the copper mines of the Congo.

NORTHER RHODESI.

ANGOLA

The colonization of Africa

For most of the 19th century, Africa consisted of many independent kingdoms. European contact was limited to a few coastal regions. At first, traders from Europe bought slaves, but later they exploited the continent's wealth of gold, diamonds, ivory, timber and other raw materials. As late as 1875, European nations controlled only about one-tenth of Africa. Twenty years later, they controlled all but one-tenth. Britain, France, Germany, Portugal, Spain and Italy took part in the 'scramble for Africa' to grab colonies for wealth and prestige. Only the freed slave state of Liberia in the west and the empire of Ethiopia in the east – the only African state to defeat a European nation – remained independent.

The Herero Uprising
An uprising by the Herero people against German rule in 1904–08 was brutally crushed.

The Boer War
From 1899 to 1902 Britain fought a vicious war against the two independent Boer republics before both were conquered.

The Great Trek
Boer farmers escaped British rule in the Cape Colony by moving north in the Great Trek of 1834–48. They settled in what became the Orange Free State and Transvaal.

SOUTHER RHODESI

gold found in Transvaal, 1886

GERMAN SOUTH-WEST AFRICA   **BECHUANALAN**

Mafe

Johannesbur

BASUTOLAND

UNION OF SOUTH AFRICA

Cape Town

Cape Colony

Egypt
Britain gained control over Egypt in 1882 after a nationalist government threatened the khedive (king) and British interests in the country.

Islamic revolt
A major Islamic revolt, in 1885, against British and Egyptian rule in the Sudan was finally put down in 1898.

Britain and France clash
A British and French confrontation at Fashoda, in 1898, over control of the Sudan, almost came to war before the conflict was settled in Britain's favour.

Adowa
Italian attempts to conquer the independent African kingdom of Ethiopia were ended at the Battle of Adowa in 1896.

ERITREA

Adowa

SUDAN

oda

FRENCH SOMALILAND

BRITISH SOMALILAND

Addis Ababa

ETHIOPIA

ITALIAN SOMALILAND

British farmer's villa, Kenya

cattle in Kenya

Lake Albert

UGANDA

Entebbe

Lake Victoria

BRITISH EAST AFRICA

Nairobi

Mombasa

Indian immigrants
Labourers were brought from British-run India to build a railroad from Mombasa on the coast up to Entebbe in Uganda.

merchant shipping

Indian Ocean

these dotted lines show the borders between states in Africa in 1914

Slave trade
The slave market in Zanzibar exported slaves to the Arab world until the British closed it down in 1873.

GERMAN EAST AFRICA

Zanzibar

nyika

Lake Malawi

NYASALAND

mbezi

alisbury

German Africa
German rule in Africa was ended during World War I, when Britain, France and South Africa occupied all of its colonies.

MOZAMBIQUE

MADAGASCAR

The Zulu Wars
Conflict between the British and the Zulu kingdom finally ended in Zulu defeat at Ulundi in 1879.

Ulundi

Limpopo

WAZILAND

Stop-over port
Merchant ships carrying tea and other products from Asia to Europe stopped off for supplies in Cape Town.

The Zulus

Shaka, leader of the Zulus of southern Africa from 1816–28, was an inspired military leader. He replaced the old thrown spear of his warriors with an *assegai*, or short stabbing spear, turning them into the most feared army in the region. The Zulus resisted all attempts by the Boers and British to take over their lands, but were finally defeated by the British at Ulundi in 1879. Unusually, the British allowed them to keep their lands, because of the respect they held for these warrior people.

Nile

Red Sea

1800

1807 British end their involvement in the transatlantic slave trade

1814 Britain gains Cape Colony from the Dutch

1822 First freed slaves settle in Liberia

1825
1826 Britain begins to take over the Gold Coast

1830 France invades Algiers
1830–1900 France conquers Algeria

1834–48 Boers move north in the Great Trek

1840–73 David Livingstone explores central Africa

1847 Liberia becomes an independent republic

1850

1852–54 Boers establish the republics of Orange Free State and Transvaal
1854 France takes over Senegal
1855 Emperor Tewedros begins to modernize Ethiopia

1861 Britain begins to colonize Nigeria

1873 British end slave market in Zanzibar
1874–76 Henry Stanley explores the Congo river region
1875
1879 British finally conquer the Zulu kingdom
1882 British take control of Egypt
1884–85 European powers divide up Africa at the Berlin Conference
1885 Leopold II of Belgium makes the Congo his personal possession
1885–98 Islamic revolt by the Mahdi against British rule in Sudan
1886 Gold discovered in the Transvaal
1888 British establish Rhodesia
1889 Italy gains Eritrea and Somaliland
1894 Britain occupies Uganda
1895 Britain occupies Kenya
1896 Italians fail to conquer Ethiopia
1898 Britain retakes Sudan
1899–1902 British defeat the Boers in South Africa
1900
1904 Britain and France settle their colonial disputes in Africa
1904–08 Herero Uprising against German rule in southwest Africa
1906 Morocco is split between France and Spain
1908 Belgium takes control of the Congo
1910 Union of South Africa gains independence from Britain

1914–18 Germany loses its African colonies during World War I

1925

Imperial Europe

In the years after 1848 the map of Europe changed considerably. Germany and Italy emerged as unified nations, and Austro-Hungary became a dual monarchy. France became an empire again and then, after 1871, a republic, while Russia slowly began to reform itself. Britain, the most powerful and richest nation in the world, avoided European entanglements and developed a vast overseas empire. In the Balkans, the Ottoman (Turkish) empire continued to fall apart, losing almost all of its European lands by 1913. The Industrial Revolution that had begun in Britain led to new industries and railways in most nations, creating new industrial towns and a large working class population.

Atlantic Ocean

The unification of Germany

In 1848 Germany consisted of 39 separate states, dominated by Prussia and Austro-Hungary. Otto von Bismarck became prime minister of Prussia in 1862. He defeated Denmark and Austria, set up a North German Confederation, excluding Austria, and took over Hanover and other German states. In 1871 Prussia defeated France and took its two eastern provinces of Alsace and Lorraine. King Wilhelm I of Prussia was then proclaimed emperor of Germany (shown above), uniting the remaining 25 German states under Prussian rule.

Gunboat diplomacy
In 1911 Germany sent a gunboat to protect its interests in Morocco, causing a major diplomatic conflict with France.

HMS Dreadnought
The battleship *Dreadnought* outclassed every other warship when she was launched in 1906, starting a naval arms race between Britain and Germany.

Queen Victoria
Queen from 1837 to 1901, Victoria was related to almost every European monarch.

North Sea

Bismarck
With a series of brilliant diplomatic and military victories, Otto von Bismarck unified Germany in 1864–71.

coal mine in the Ruhr valley, Germany

Karl Marx
The communist revolutionary Karl Marx fled Germany and took refuge in London in 1848.

Revolution
In 1848 the unpopular King Louis-Philippe was overthrown and France became a republic, a nation not governed by a monarch.

a barricade erected in Paris

Napoleon III
Nephew of Napoleon Bonaparte, Louis Napoleon became president of France in 1848 before seizing power and becoming emperor in 1851.

free trade in northern Germany

armaments factory in Pilsen

French farmers

Emmanuel II
King of Sardinia since 1849, Victor Emmanuel II became king of a united Italy in 1860.

NORWAY
OSLO

COPENHAGEN
DENMARK
Schleswig-Holstein

GERMAN EMP
BERL
Rhine
Elbe
Pils

BRITAIN
LONDON
NETHERLANDS
BELGIUM
Sedan Frankfurt
LUXEMBOURG
PARIS
Alsace-Lorraine
SWITZERLAND ALPS
FRANCE

ITALY
Corsica
ROME
Sardinia

PORTUGAL
MADRID
SPAIN
Balearic Islands

Pyrenees

Mediterranean Sea

MOROCCO

0   500 km
0   250 miles

Industrial revolution
In the second half of the 19th century, Russia industrialized very quickly, opening many new coal mines, steel works and factories.

EDEN
STOCKHOLM

Sadowa
In the Seven Weeks' War of 1866, Prussia defeated Austria at Sadowa and ended the country's influence in Germany.

MOSCOW

Trans-continental railway
The Trans-Siberian Railway linking Moscow to Vladivostok, on the Pacific coast, was begun in 1891 but not finished until 1916.

Freedom
Serfs (peasants) in Russia received their freedom from their owners in 1861.

The Dual Monarchy
In 1867 the Austrian empire split into a two-monarch state called 'Austro-Hungary'. United by its Habsburg rulers, it had a common army and currency.

RUSSIAN EMPIRE

Ukraine
Ukraine was the 'bread basket of Russia', as well as its major industrial area.

wheat being harvested in the Ukraine

Potemkin
Revolution broke out in Russia in 1905 and spread to the armed forces. The crew of the Russian battleship *Potemkin* mutinied and fled to Romania.

dowa
Koniggratz)

VIENNA

AUSTRO-HUNGARIAN EMPIRE

Danube

Odessa

Black Sea

ROMANIA
Ploesti
BUCHAREST

Romanian oil
Before the development of Middle Eastern oil, most European oil came from the oil wells of Ploesti.

Bosnia **SERBIA**
Balkans
BULGARIA
SOFIA

MONTENEGRO

Constantinople

OTTOMAN EMPIRE

Albania

The Balkan Wars
Two wars in the Balkans in 1912–13 saw the Ottoman Turks almost expelled from Europe, while Serbia emerged as a major Balkan nation.

GREECE
ATHENS

Rhodes
Cyprus

Garibaldi
In 1859–60 the Italian nationalist Giuseppe Garibaldi invaded Sicily and Naples with 1,000 troops, and forced them to unify with the rest of Italy.

Crete

The Royal Navy
The British Royal Navy commanded the Mediterranean, protecting British sea routes to India.

Mediterranean Sea

these dotted lines show the borders between European nations in 1912

EGYPT

1840

1848 Revolutions in France, Italy, Germany and Austria against conservative rule
1848 Karl Marx flees to London
1849 Attempts to set up a German National Assembly end in failure

1850

1851 Napoleon III seizes power in France and restores the French empire

1859–60 Italian kingdoms united as one nation under Victor Emmanuel II

1860

1861 Russian serfs (peasants) liberated
1862 Bismarck becomes prime minister of Prussia
1863–64 Prussia defeats Denmark to gain two northern duchies
1866 Seven Weeks' War
1866 Italy gains Venice from Austria
1867 Creation of North German Confederation under Prussian rule
1867 Creation of Austro-Hungary

1870

1870 Italy takes over the Papal States to complete its unification
1870–71 Franco-Prussian war ends in French defeat; creation of German empire
1871 Third Republic established in France
1878 Romania gains independence from the Ottoman empire
1878 Britain gains Cyprus from Ottomans
1879–82 Triple Alliance of Germany, Austro-Hungary and Italy

1880

1883 Death of Karl Marx

1888 Wilhelm II becomes emperor of Germany

1890
1890 Bismarck resigns

1894 Franco-Russian military alliance

1900
1901 Death of Queen Victoria

1904 Entente Cordiale ('friendly understanding') agreement between Britain and France
1906 HMS 'Dreadnought' launched; naval arms race begins in Europe
1908 Austro-Hungary takes over Bosnia
1908 Bulgaria becomes independent

1910

1912–13 Two Balkan wars redraw the map of southeast Europe
1913 Albania becomes an independent nation
1914 World War I breaks out in Europe

1920

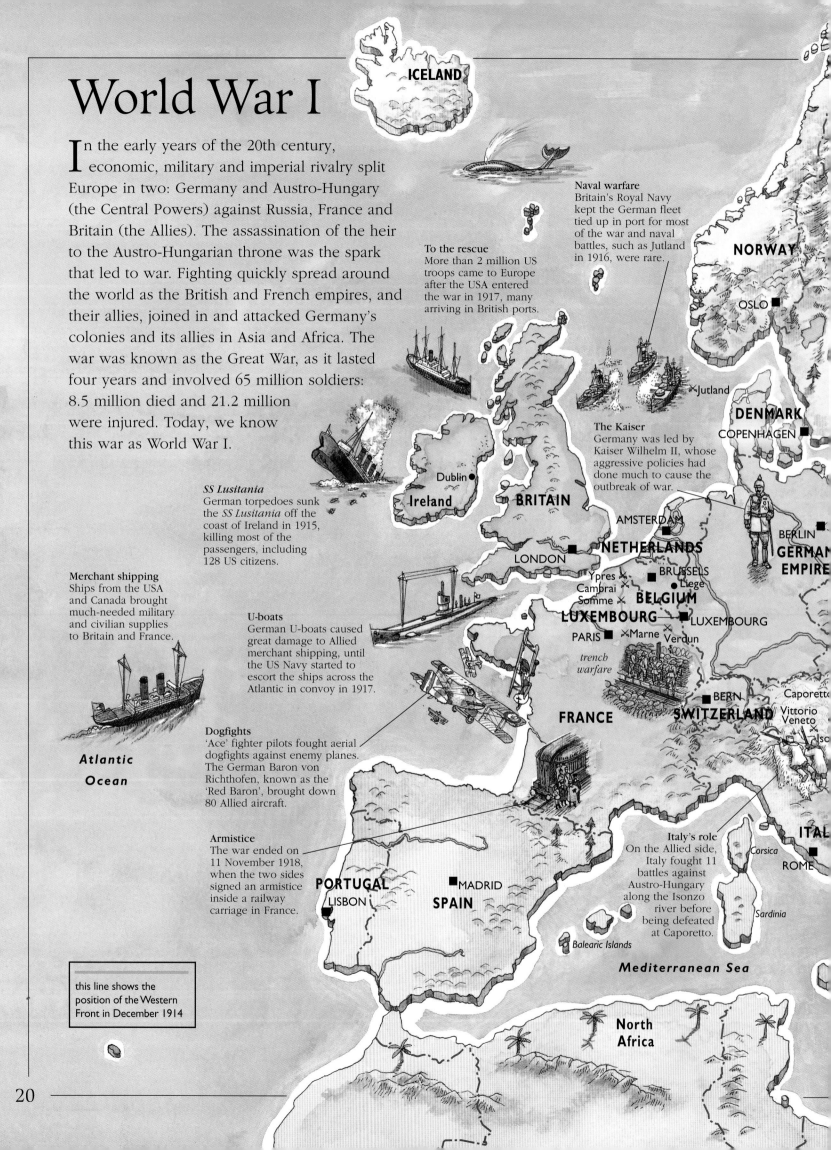

World War I

In the early years of the 20th century, economic, military and imperial rivalry split Europe in two: Germany and Austro-Hungary (the Central Powers) against Russia, France and Britain (the Allies). The assassination of the heir to the Austro-Hungarian throne was the spark that led to war. Fighting quickly spread around the world as the British and French empires, and their allies, joined in and attacked Germany's colonies and its allies in Asia and Africa. The war was known as the Great War, as it lasted four years and involved 65 million soldiers: 8.5 million died and 21.2 million were injured. Today, we know this war as World War I.

ICELAND

To the rescue
More than 2 million US troops came to Europe after the USA entered the war in 1917, many arriving in British ports.

Naval warfare
Britain's Royal Navy kept the German fleet tied up in port for most of the war and naval battles, such as Jutland in 1916, were rare.

✕ Jutland

NORWAY

OSLO ■

DENMARK
COPENHAGEN ■

The Kaiser
Germany was led by Kaiser Wilhelm II, whose aggressive policies had done much to cause the outbreak of war.

SS Lusitania
German torpedoes sunk the *SS Lusitania* off the coast of Ireland in 1915, killing most of the passengers, including 128 US citizens.

Dublin ●

Ireland

BRITAIN

AMSTERDAM ■
NETHERLANDS
LONDON ■
BRUSSELS ■
Ypres ✕
Cambrai ✕ ● Liège
Somme ✕ **BELGIUM**
LUXEMBOURG ■ LUXEMBOURG
PARIS ■ ✕ Marne ✕ Verdun

BERLIN ■
GERMAN EMPIRE

Merchant shipping
Ships from the USA and Canada brought much-needed military and civilian supplies to Britain and France.

U-boats
German U-boats caused great damage to Allied merchant shipping, until the US Navy started to escort the ships across the Atlantic in convoy in 1917.

trench warfare

BERN ■
SWITZERLAND

Caporetto

Vittorio Veneto ✕
Iso...

ITAL...

Atlantic Ocean

Dogfights
'Ace' fighter pilots fought aerial dogfights against enemy planes. The German Baron von Richthofen, known as the 'Red Baron', brought down 80 Allied aircraft.

FRANCE

Armistice
The war ended on 11 November 1918, when the two sides signed an armistice inside a railway carriage in France.

Italy's role
On the Allied side, Italy fought 11 battles against Austro-Hungary along the Isonzo river before being defeated at Caporetto.

Corsica

ROME ■

PORTUGAL
LISBON ■

■ MADRID
SPAIN

Sardinia

Balearic Islands

Mediterranean Sea

this line shows the position of the Western Front in December 1914

North Africa

Tsar
The Russian tsar Nicholas II was a poor military leader who lost the support of his people during the war. He was overthrown in the revolution of 1917.

HELSINKI

Finland

EDEN

STOCKHOLM

ST PETERSBURG (PETROGRAD)

Moscow

RUSSIAN EMPIRE

The Eastern Front
Unlike the stalemate in the west, the war in the east was very mobile, with large-scale battles and troops advancing over hundreds of kilometres.

Masurian Lakes

Tannenberg

Russians marching into Austro-Hungary

Peace treaty
After two revolutions in 1917, the new Bolshevik (communist) rulers of Russia made peace with Germany at Brest-Litovsk.

Brest-Litovsk

War production
Both sides in the war produced vast amounts of shells and other armaments in munitions factories placed well behind the front line.

AUSTRO-HUNGARIAN EMPIRE

BUDAPEST

ROMANIA

BUCHAREST

BELGRADE

Sarajevo

SERBIA

BULGARIA

SOFIA

MONTENEGRO

Black Sea

Trench warfare
The worst fighting took place along the Western Front in western Europe. Each side dug a long line of defensive trenches facing the enemy. They regularly bombarded the opposing side and launched attacks over the top of the trenches, at huge cost to human life. Neither side made any real progress until late in 1918, when fresh American troops and improved artillery bombardment gave the Allies the advantage.

0   500 km
0   250 miles

Genocide
During 1915 the Ottomans deported Armenians from their homeland to stop them helping the Russians. Up to 1.3 million were killed.

Armenia

CONSTANTINOPLE

Gallipoli

OTTOMAN EMPIRE

Lawrence of Arabia
In 1916 the Arabs rose in revolt against their Ottoman rulers, supported by the British officer T E Lawrence, in the hope of winning their independence.

TIRANA
ALBANIA

GREECE

ATHENS

Assassination
The assassination of Archduke Franz Ferdinand, heir to the Austrian throne, by Serb nationalist Gavrilo Princip sparked the outbreak of the war.

Malta

Crete

Gallipoli
Allied landings on the Gallipoli peninsula in the Ottoman empire were a disaster and the troops were forced to withdraw.

Cyprus

Mediterranean Sea

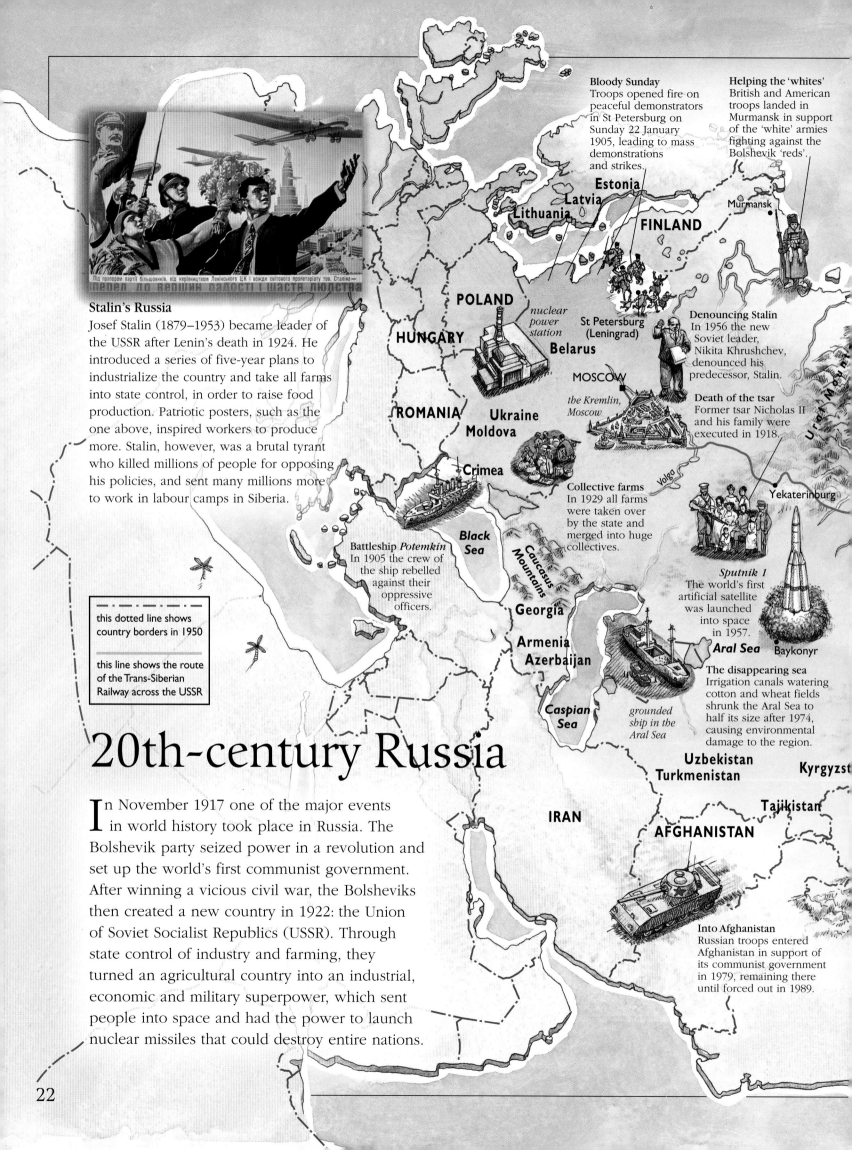

Bloody Sunday
Troops opened fire on peaceful demonstrators in St Petersburg on Sunday 22 January 1905, leading to mass demonstrations and strikes.

Helping the 'whites'
British and American troops landed in Murmansk in support of the 'white' armies fighting against the Bolshevik 'reds'.

Stalin's Russia
Josef Stalin (1879–1953) became leader of the USSR after Lenin's death in 1924. He introduced a series of five-year plans to industrialize the country and take all farms into state control, in order to raise food production. Patriotic posters, such as the one above, inspired workers to produce more. Stalin, however, was a brutal tyrant who killed millions of people for opposing his policies, and sent many millions more to work in labour camps in Siberia.

Denouncing Stalin
In 1956 the new Soviet leader, Nikita Khrushchev, denounced his predecessor, Stalin.

Death of the tsar
Former tsar Nicholas II and his family were executed in 1918.

Collective farms
In 1929 all farms were taken over by the state and merged into huge collectives.

Sputnik 1
The world's first artificial satellite was launched into space in 1957.

The disappearing sea
Irrigation canals watering cotton and wheat fields shrunk the Aral Sea to half its size after 1974, causing environmental damage to the region.

Into Afghanistan
Russian troops entered Afghanistan in support of its communist government in 1979, remaining there until forced out in 1989.

Battleship *Potemkin*
In 1905 the crew of the ship rebelled against their oppressive officers.

this dotted line shows country borders in 1950

this line shows the route of the Trans-Siberian Railway across the USSR

Estonia
Latvia
Lithuania
FINLAND
Murmansk
POLAND
nuclear power station
St Petersburg (Leningrad)
HUNGARY
Belarus
MOSCOW
the Kremlin, Moscow
ROMANIA
Ukraine
Moldova
Crimea
Volga
Yekaterinburg
Black Sea
Caucasus Mountains
Georgia
Armenia
Azerbaijan
Aral Sea
Baykonyr
grounded ship in the Aral Sea
Caspian Sea
Uzbekistan
Turkmenistan
Kyrgyzst
Tajikistan
IRAN
AFGHANISTAN

20th-century Russia

In November 1917 one of the major events in world history took place in Russia. The Bolshevik party seized power in a revolution and set up the world's first communist government. After winning a vicious civil war, the Bolsheviks then created a new country in 1922: the Union of Soviet Socialist Republics (USSR). Through state control of industry and farming, they turned an agricultural country into an industrial, economic and military superpower, which sent people into space and had the power to launch nuclear missiles that could destroy entire nations.

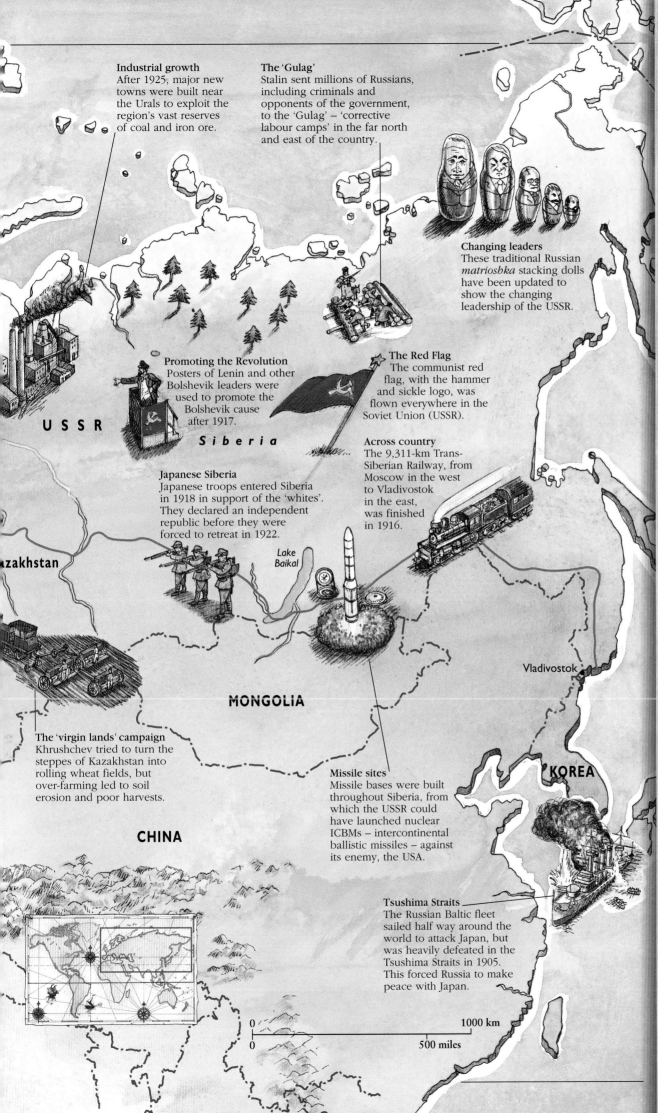

Industrial growth
After 1925, major new towns were built near the Urals to exploit the region's vast reserves of coal and iron ore.

The 'Gulag'
Stalin sent millions of Russians, including criminals and opponents of the government, to the 'Gulag' – 'corrective labour camps' in the far north and east of the country.

Changing leaders
These traditional Russian *matrioshka* stacking dolls have been updated to show the changing leadership of the USSR.

Promoting the Revolution
Posters of Lenin and other Bolshevik leaders were used to promote the Bolshevik cause after 1917.

The Red Flag
The communist red flag, with the hammer and sickle logo, was flown everywhere in the Soviet Union (USSR).

U S S R

S i b e r i a

Japanese Siberia
Japanese troops entered Siberia in 1918 in support of the 'whites'. They declared an independent republic before they were forced to retreat in 1922.

Across country
The 9,311-km Trans-Siberian Railway, from Moscow in the west to Vladivostok in the east, was finished in 1916.

Lake Baikal

zakhstan

MONGOLIA

The 'virgin lands' campaign
Khrushchev tried to turn the steppes of Kazakhstan into rolling wheat fields, but over-farming led to soil erosion and poor harvests.

Vladivostok

CHINA

Missile sites
Missile bases were built throughout Siberia, from which the USSR could have launched nuclear ICBMs – intercontinental ballistic missiles – against its enemy, the USA.

KOREA

Tsushima Straits
The Russian Baltic fleet sailed half way around the world to attack Japan, but was heavily defeated in the Tsushima Straits in 1905. This forced Russia to make peace with Japan.

0   1000 km

0   500 miles

1900–1990

1900

1904–05 Russia is heavily defeated by Japan and loses land in the east
1905 Revolution breaks out across Russia

1910
1914 Russia enters World War I against Germany and Austro-Hungary
1917 Tsar Nicholas II abdicates in March
1917 Bolsheviks seize power in November
1918 Treaty of Brest-Litovsk ends war for Russia
1918–21 Civil war between 'reds' and 'whites'; western troops help 'whites'
1918 Bolsheviks murder Nicholas II and family

1920
1920–22 Peasant revolts occur across Russia
1921 'New economic policy' re-introduces free trade to encourage food production
1922 Union of Soviet Socialist Republics (USSR) is set up
1924 Death of Lenin; Stalin takes over as leader
1928 First 'Five Year Plan' introduced to industrialize the country
1929 Collectivization of farms begins
1930

1932–33 Massive famine in Ukraine and central Asia as a result of collectivization
1934 Stalin begins show trials and 'purges' to get rid of opponents

1938 Stalin's purges at their worst
1939 Nazi-Soviet Pact with Hitler
1940
1941 Germany invades the USSR during World War II

1945 Soviet troops enter Berlin at the end of World War II

1949 USSR explodes its first atomic bomb
1950
1953 Death of Stalin; Khrushchev takes over as leader
1954 'Virgin lands' policy launched to grow more crops
1956 Khrushchev denounces (fiercely criticizes) Stalin in a secret speech
1957 USSR launches 'Sputnik I', the world's first man-made satellite, into space

1960
1961 Soviet cosmonaut Yuri Gagarin becomes the first person in space

1964 Khrushchev ousted; Leonid Brezhnev takes over as leader

1970

1972 US president Nixon visits the USSR

1979 Russian troops enter Afghanistan
1980

1982 Death of Brezhnev; Yuri Andropov and then Konstantin Chernenko succeed him

1985 Mikhail Gorbachev becomes leader of the USSR and begins reforms

1990

America and the Great Depression:
Economic boom and bust

The US economic boom of the 1920s ended when the New York Stock Exchange crashed in October 1929. As prices and profits collapsed and banks failed, the USA – and then the world – entered a decade-long economic slump. Millions of people lost their jobs or had their incomes reduced, while world trade was cut by almost two-thirds between 1929 and 1932. In the USA, President Roosevelt's New Deal tried to tackle the problem, but it was the threat of war in Europe and Asia, and the need to make more weapons, that finally produced the jobs that got the unemployed back to work.

The post-war boom

The 1920s were a period of great optimism in America. The economy was booming after World War I, the country was peaceful and prosperous, and women had more freedom than ever before. New forms of entertainment, such as the movies and jazz music, transformed the lives of ordinary people. The picture above shows fashionable women of the 1920s, known as flappers, who summed up the spirit of the decade. Many thought the boom would last for ever.

Hollywood

The invention of a workable sound movie system in 1927 transformed the cinema, killing off silent films by 1930. Millions of people flocked to the cinema during the 1930s to see spectacular films, such as *The Wizard of Oz* (below), and take their minds off the economic gloom of their daily lives.

Worldwide slump

The economic slump began in the USA but had spread around the world by 1931. As millions lost their jobs, social and political unrest grew. In Britain, in 1936, 200 unemployed shipyard workers from Jarrow in northeast England marched south to London to draw attention to the poverty and lack of jobs in their town.

The New Deal

In 1933 Franklin D Roosevelt, pictured here (right), became president, pledging 'a new deal for the American people'. He reformed the banking system, gave financial support to farmers and home owners and, through the Public Works Administration, set millions of people to work building dams, roads, bridges, schools and other public projects.

Extreme poverty

Unemployment in the USA rose from 2 million industrial workers in 1928 to 11.6 million in 1932, and stayed high for the rest of the decade. Millions of people lost their life savings when their banks failed. They were forced to rely on soup kitchens (below) and money from the government to keep them alive. In 1934–38, extreme poverty spread to the farming communities of Oklahoma, Kansas and other mid-western states when high winds stripped a huge area of land of its soil.

Europe between the World Wars

The years after World War I were chaotic across the whole of Europe. Germany tried to recover from its defeat in the war. Meanwhile new countries, which had emerged from the former defeated empires, struggled to establish themselves as independent states. Economic chaos after the slump of 1931 only made matters worse as millions were thrown out of work. Fascist (extreme right-wing and dictatorial) parties came to power in Italy, much of eastern Europe and, in 1933, Germany. This divided the continent between democracies, dictatorships, and the USSR, which was a dictatorship and the world's only communist state.

Atlantic Ocean

The Spanish Civil War

In 1936 the Spanish army, led by the Nationalist General Franco, rose in revolt against the democratic Republican government. The civil war that followed lasted three years and involved many international forces: the USSR sent arms to the Republicans, Germany and Italy sent troops and planes to the Nationalist rebels, volunteers from around the world fought on both sides, while Britain and France remained neutral. The war ended with a Nationalist victory in 1939, starting 36 years of authoritarian government in Spain.

Free Ireland
After centuries of British rule, most of Ireland became an independent nation in 1921.

Television
The first regular TV broadcasts in Europe were made by the British Broadcasting Corporation (BBC) in 1936.

North Sea

Hyper-inflation
German economic collapse in 1923 caused such massive inflation that trillions of marks were needed just to buy simple groceries.

Jews fleeing the Nazis

'Peace in our time'
In 1938 the British prime minister, Neville Chamberlain, returned from Germany believing he had reached a peace settlement with Hitler.

Versailles
The leaders of the four victorious Allied powers met at Versailles, outside Paris, to agree the peace settlement with Germany after World War I.

Guernica
In April 1937 German bombers destroyed the ancient Basque capital during the Spanish Civil War.

Unemployed
The huge rise in unemployment, after the 1931 worldwide economic slump, led to massive social unrest.

Two dictators
Hitler and Mussolini agreed an alliance – the Rome-Berlin Axis – in 1936. Other countries joined the Axis during World War II.

Civil war
Up to one million people lost their lives during the civil war in Spain.

NORWAY
OSLO

DENMARK

NETHERLANDS
AMSTERDAM
BRUSSELS
BELGIUM
LONDON
Rhine
Rhineland

BRITAIN
DUBLIN
IRISH FREE STATE

PARIS
Nuremberg rally

SWITZERLAND
BERN

FRANCE

Guernica
Basque Country

SPAIN
MADRID

PORTUGAL
LISBON

Corsica
Sardinia
Balearic Islands

Mediterranean Sea

FINLAND

HELSINKI

SWEDEN

STOCKHOLM

TALLINN

ESTONIA

RIGA

LATVIA

PENHAGEN

LITHUANIA

East Prussia

DANZIG

The USSR
As the world's only communist state, the USSR under Stalin largely stayed out of European politics. It watched the rise of Hitler with alarm, before allying with him in 1939.

MOSCOW

U S S R

BERLIN

GERMANY

WARSAW

The Polish Corridor
The thin strip of land giving Poland access to the Baltic Sea contained many Germans and was a source of tension between the two countries.

Starvation
Under Josef Stalin, millions of peasants starved as their farms were taken under state control.

Communist Hungary
The Communists under Bela Kun seized power in Hungary in 1919, but were quickly forced out by an invading Romanian army.

POLAND

udetenland

RAGUE

CZECHOSLOVAKIA

ich

VIENNA

STRIA

BUDAPEST

HUNGARY

Union
In March 1938 Germany occupied Austria, causing the *Anschluss* – the union of both countries.

German troops in Austria

ROMANIA

BUCHAREST

BELGRADE

Danube

Black Sea

YUGOSLAVIA

BULGARIA

SOFIA

Ataturk
Kemal Ataturk, a World War I hero, abolished the Turkish sultanate in 1922 and set up an independent republic in 1923.

ALY

ROME

TIRANA

ALBANIA

TURKEY

Greek immigration
More than 1 million Greeks were forced to flee Asia Minor when Turkey occupied some Greek cities in 1922.

GREECE

ATHENS

Cyprus

Yugoslavia
Yugoslavia became one country in 1919, merging the Serb, Croat and Slovene peoples into one state.

Sicily

Crete

Mediterranean Sea

Mussolini
Mussolini and his Fascist Party took power in Italy in 1922 and soon crushed all opposition to their rule.

0   500 km

0   250 miles

1910–1940

1910

1918 World War I ends with the defeat of Germany and Austro-Hungary

1919–20 Treaty of Versailles, and other peace treaties, are signed in France to draw up the post-war borders of Europe

1919 Yugoslavia, Hungary, Czechoslovakia, Poland, Finland and three Baltic states (Estonia, Latvia and Lithuania) emerge from the ruins of the Austro-Hungarian and Russian empires

1920

1920 Communists try to take power in Germany

1920–21 Poland wins war against the USSR

1921 Irish Free State established within the British empire

1922 Mussolini takes power in Italy

1922 Greeks expelled from Asia Minor

1922 Germany and the USSR sign an economic treaty

1923 Turkish republic set up under Kemal Ataturk

1926 General Strike in Britain

1928 Kellogg-Briand Pact signed in Paris: all nations agree to renounce war

1929 Beginning of the Great Depression

1930

1931 Worldwide economic slump

1931 Spain becomes a republic

1933 Adolf Hitler comes to power in Germany

1934 Greece, Romania, Turkey and Yugoslavia sign the Balkan Pact against Germany and the USSR

1935–36 Italy invades Abyssinia (Ethiopia)

1936 British Broadcasting Corporation (BBC) begins regular TV broadcasts

1936 Germany re-occupies the demilitarized Rhineland

1936 Germany and Italy agree the Rome-Berlin Axis alliance

1936–39 Spanish Civil War

1938 Germany takes over Austria

1938 Germany takes Sudetenland from Czechoslovakia after Britain, France and Italy agree terms with Germany in Munich

1939 Germany takes over the rest of Czechoslovakia

1939 Italy occupies Albania

1939 Nazi-Soviet pact: Germany and Russia agree to partition (split up) Poland

1939 Germany invades Poland, beginning World War II

1940

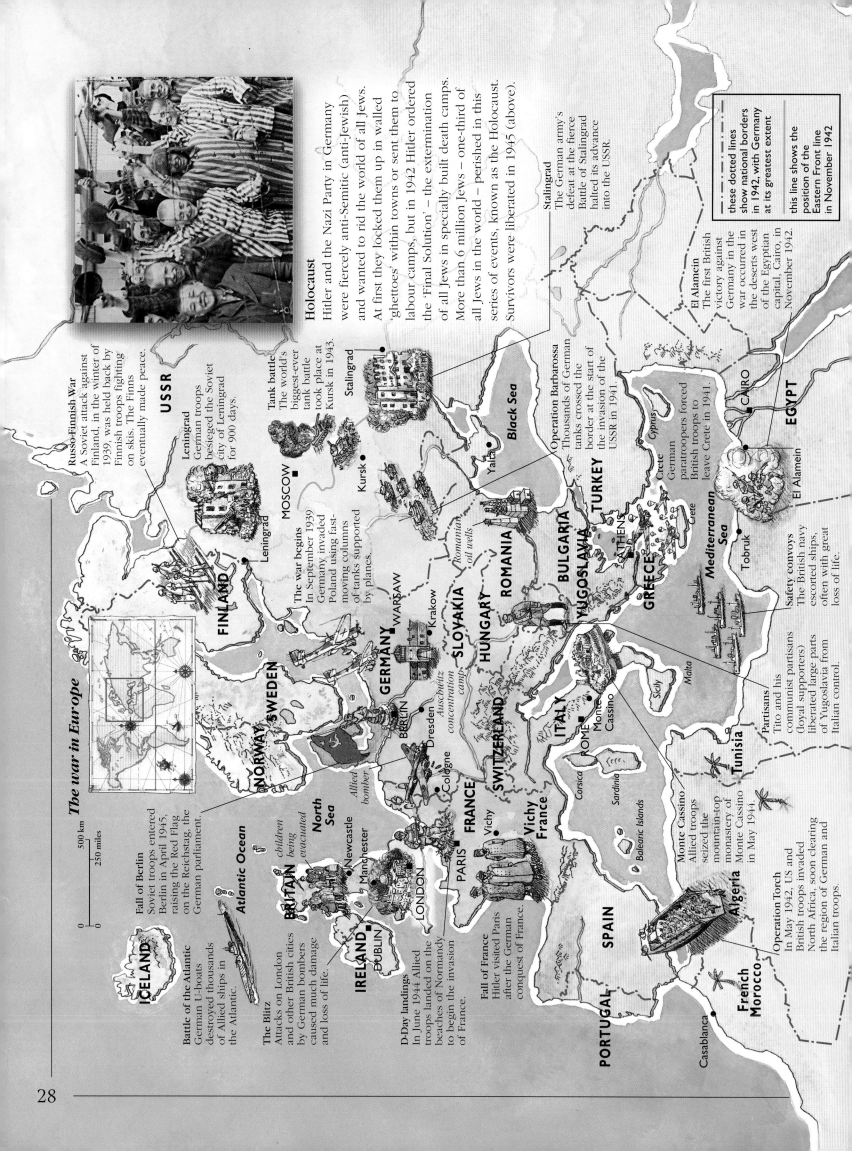

The war in Europe

Holocaust
Hitler and the Nazi Party in Germany were fiercely anti-Semitic (anti-Jewish) and wanted to rid the world of all Jews. At first they locked them up in walled 'ghettoes' within towns or sent them to labour camps, but in 1942 Hitler ordered the 'Final Solution' – the extermination of all Jews in specially built death camps. More than 6 million Jews – one-third of all Jews in the world – perished in this series of events, known as the Holocaust. Survivors were liberated in 1945 (above).

Stalingrad
The German army's defeat at the fierce Battle of Stalingrad halted its advance into the USSR.

El Alamein
The first British victory against Germany in the war occurred in the deserts west of the Egyptian capital, Cairo, in November 1942.

---

these dotted lines show national borders in 1942, with Germany at its greatest extent

this line shows the position of the Eastern Front line in November 1942

Russo-Finnish War
A Soviet attack against Finland, in the winter of 1939, was held back by Finnish troops fighting on skis. The Finns eventually made peace.

Leningrad
German troops besieged the Soviet city of Leningrad for 900 days.

Tank battle
The world's biggest-ever tank battle took place at Kursk in 1943.

The war begins
In September 1939 Germany invaded Poland using fast-moving columns of tanks supported by planes.

Operation Barbarossa
Thousands of German tanks crossed the border at the start of the invasion of the USSR in 1941.

Crete
German paratroopers forced British troops to leave Crete in 1941.

Safety convoys
The British navy escorted ships, often with great loss of life.

Partisans
Tito and his communist partisans (loyal supporters) liberated large parts of Yugoslavia from Italian control.

Monte Cassino
Allied troops seized the mountain-top monastery of Monte Cassino in May 1944.

Operation Torch
In May 1942, US and British troops invaded North Africa, soon clearing the region of German and Italian troops.

Fall of France
Hitler visited Paris after the German conquest of France.

D-Day landings
In June 1944 Allied troops landed on the beaches of Normandy to begin the invasion of France.

The Blitz
Attacks on London and other British cities by German bombers caused much damage and loss of life.

Battle of the Atlantic
German U-boats destroyed thousands of Allied ships in the Atlantic.

Fall of Berlin
Soviet troops entered Berlin in April 1945, raising the Red Flag on the Reichstag, the German parliament.

ICELAND

Atlantic Ocean

North Sea

children being evacuated

BRITAIN
Newcastle
Manchester
IRELAND
DUBLIN
LONDON

NORWAY
SWEDEN
FINLAND
Leningrad

USSR
MOSCOW
Kursk
Yalta

Black Sea

Stalingrad

GERMANY
BERLIN
Dresden
Cologne
Allied bomber
WARSAW
Krakow
Auschwitz concentration camp

SLOVAKIA
HUNGARY
ROMANIA
Romanian oil wells

FRANCE
PARIS
Vichy
Vichy France
SWITZERLAND

SPAIN
PORTUGAL
Casablanca
French Morocco
Algeria
Tunisia

ITALY
ROME
Monte Cassino
Corsica
Sardinia
Balearic Islands
Sicily
Malta

BULGARIA
YUGOSLAVIA
GREECE
ATHENS
TURKEY
Crete
Cyprus

Mediterranean Sea
Tobruk
EGYPT
CAIRO
El Alamein

0   500 km
0   250 miles

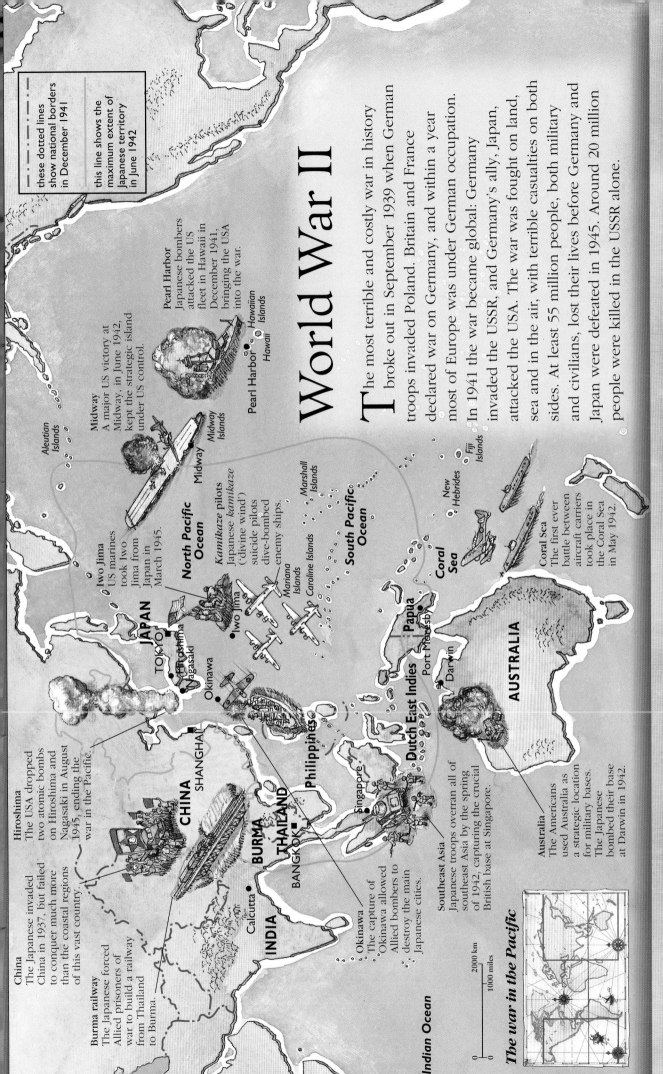

World War II

The most terrible and costly war in history broke out in September 1939 when German troops invaded Poland. Britain and France declared war on Germany, and within a year most of Europe was under German occupation. In 1941 the war became global: Germany invaded the USSR, and Germany's ally, Japan, attacked the USA. The war was fought on land, sea and in the air, with terrible casualties on both sides. At least 55 million people, both military and civilians, lost their lives before Germany and Japan were defeated in 1945. Around 20 million people were killed in the USSR alone.

these dotted lines show national borders in December 1941

this line shows the maximum extent of Japanese territory in June 1942

Pearl Harbor
Japanese bombers attacked the US fleet in Hawaii in December 1941, bringing the USA into the war.

Midway
A major US victory at Midway, in June 1942, kept the strategic island under US control.

Aleutian Islands

Hawaiian Islands
Hawaii

Pearl Harbor

Midway
Midway Islands

North Pacific Ocean

Kamikaze pilots
Japanese *kamikaze* ('divine wind') suicide pilots dive-bombed enemy ships.

Marshall Islands

Caroline Islands

Mariana Islands

South Pacific Ocean

Fiji Islands

New Hebrides

Iwo Jima
US marines took Iwo Jima from Japan in March 1945.

Iwo Jima

JAPAN

TOKYO
Hiroshima
Nagasaki
Okinawa

Hiroshima
The USA dropped two atomic bombs on Hiroshima and Nagasaki in August 1945, ending the war in the Pacific.

Burma railway
The Japanese forced Allied prisoners of war to build a railway from Thailand to Burma.

China
The Japanese invaded China in 1937, but failed to conquer much more than the coastal regions of this vast country.

CHINA
SHANGHAI

BURMA
THAILAND
BANGKOK

INDIA
Calcutta

Singapore
Philippines

Dutch East Indies

Port Moresby
Papua

Darwin

Coral Sea
Coral Sea
The first ever battle between aircraft carriers took place in the Coral Sea in May 1942.

AUSTRALIA

Okinawa
The capture of Okinawa allowed Allied bombers to destroy the main Japanese cities.

Southeast Asia
Japanese troops overran all of southeast Asia by the spring of 1942, capturing the crucial British base at Singapore.

Australia
The Americans used Australia as a strategic location for military bases. The Japanese bombed their base at Darwin in 1942.

The war in the Pacific

Indian Ocean

2000 km
1000 miles
0
0

1939–1946

1939
Sept Germany invades Poland; Britain and France declare war – start of World War II
Nov USSR invades Finland

1940
April Germany invades Denmark and Norway
May Germany invades the Low Countries and France
June Italy enters the war on Germany's side
July–Oct Battle of Britain: the British air force defeats the German Luftwaffe (air force)
Sept Blitz against British cities begins
Sept Italians invade Egypt
Oct Italians invade Greece
Oct Hungary, Romania and Bulgaria join Germany and Italy

1941
April Germany invades Yugoslavia and Greece
May British are forced out of Crete
June Operation Barbarossa: Germany invades the USSR
Sept Siege of Leningrad begins
Dec Japan attacks Pearl Harbor; the USA enters the war
Dec German advance stopped outside Moscow

1942
Jan Hitler orders the extermination of all Jews
Feb–Mar Japanese bomb Darwin; Japanese take Malaya, Singapore and the Dutch East Indies
April–May Battle of the Coral Sea halts the Japanese advance
May Japanese take the Philippines
May First British area-bombing campaign against Cologne
Oct–Nov British victory at El Alamein, Egypt
Nov Operation Torch: Allied invasion of North Africa
Nov Germans occupy Vichy France

1943
Feb Germans surrender at Stalingrad
April Jewish uprising in Warsaw, Poland
May Battle of the Atlantic ends
May German and Italian troops surrender in Tunisia
June–Aug Soviets defeat German tanks at Kursk
July Allies invade Italy

1944
Jan Siege of Leningrad ends
June D-Day: Allied troops invade France
June Allies begin their bombing of southern Japan from Chinese bases
July Soviet troops enter Poland
Aug Allied troops liberate Paris
Oct British troops liberate Greece
Oct Battle of Leyte Gulf in the Philippines ends Japanese naval power
Nov First Japanese 'kamikaze' attacks on Allied ships

1945
Mar Allied troops cross the River Rhine
Mar US marines take Iwo Jima in the Pacific
April Soviet troops enter Berlin
April Hitler commits suicide
May Italy and Germany surrender: peace in Europe
May US marines take Okinawa and begin to bomb Japan
May Allied firestorm devastates Tokyo
Aug USA drops atomic bombs on Hiroshima and Nagasaki; Soviets attack Japan
Sept Japanese surrender: the war ends

1946

The Cold War

The USA and USSR emerged victorious at the end of World War II, but political differences between them soon erupted into a 'cold' war – one that never reached an all-out military conflict, despite the ever-present threat of war. By 1949 the world was roughly divided between pro-western and pro-communist states. Allies of the two sides fought wars on their behalf, such as in Korea and Vietnam, while both the USSR and USA built up huge arsenals of nuclear and other weapons. Attempts to achieve an understanding between the two sides failed in the 1970s. By the late 1980s, the USA had out-spent the USSR and forced it towards financial ruin. The collapse of communism brought the Cold War to an end in 1991.

American firepower
In the 1980s the USA was able to out-spend the USSR on nuclear weaponry, leading to a series of arms reduction agreements in 1988 and 1991.

The United Nations
Many of the Cold War diplomatic meetings took place at the UN headquarters in New York City.

Greenham Common
The decision to place US nuclear missiles in Britain, in 1982, led to huge protests at the Greenham Common base. The missiles were removed in 1989.

The Cuban missile crisis
In 1962 the USSR stationed nuclear missiles on Cuba, bringing the world to the brink of nuclear war before they agreed to remove them.

Guatemala
In 1954 the USA backed a counter-revolution in Guatemala to overthrow the socialist government and install a pro-USA, military government.

Grenada
In 1983 US troops overthrew the left-wing (socialist) government of Grenada, because of its growing ties with communist Cuba.

Nicaragua
In 1978 the radical Sandinista rebels overthrew the military government and introduced many social reforms. This led to a lengthy civil war until peace was declared in 1990.

Chile
In 1973 a US-backed military coup overthrew President Allende, the world's first democratically elected Marxist head of state.

CANADA

UNITED STATES OF AMERICA

Fulton

New York

WASHINGTON D.C.

CUBA

GUATEMALA

NICARAGUA

GRENADA

CHILE

SANTIAGO

Reykjavik

WEST GERMANY

BRITAIN

Greenham Common

LONDON

PARIS

Geneva

FRANCE

SPAIN

Pacific Ocean

Atlantic Ocean

these dotted lines show the borders between nations in 1949

| 0 | 4000 km |
| 0 | 2000 miles |

The end of the Cold War
After 1985 the new leader of the USSR, Mikhail Gorbachev, wanted to reduce military spending and improve the living conditions of Soviet citizens. In 1988 he pulled Soviet troops out of eastern Europe. Without Soviet support, the communist governments there could not survive. One by one, democratically elected governments replaced them. In 1989 a hated symbol of the Cold War, the Berlin Wall (left), was pulled down. One year later, Germany was reunited as one nation. By then the USSR was collapsing, and was replaced by 15 independent nations in 1991.

The Berlin Wall
In 1961 communist authorities in East Berlin erected a wall to prevent its citizens fleeing to freedom in the west.

The USA–USSR arms race
The development of intercontinental ballistic missiles in the 1960s led to an expensive race to build up arms.

Mikhail Gorbachev
In 1985 Gorbachev became leader of the USSR and introduced much-needed social and economic reforms.

Divided Korea
In 1950 communist North Korea invaded capitalist South Korea. A ceasefire was agreed, but the peninsula remains divided.

UNION OF SOVIET SOCIALIST REPUBLICS

■MOSCOW

■WARSAW
EAST GERMANY
■PRAGUE
CZECHOSLOVAKIA
■BUDAPEST

The 'Prague Spring'
An attempt to soften the communist rule in Czechoslovakia was crushed by Soviet and other troops in 1968.

Chairman Mao
Mao Zedong led communist China from 1949 until his death in 1976.

HUNGARY

SYRIA

LEBANON

IRAQ

ISRAEL

IRAN

AFGHANISTAN

CHINA

NORTH KOREA

Hungary
In 1956 Soviet tanks crushed Hungary's attempt to pull out of the pro-Soviet Warsaw Pact.

EGYPT JORDAN

INDIA

The Vietnam War
In the war of 1954–75, the USA supported South Vietnam. The USSR and China supported communist North Vietnam, the eventual victor.

SOUTH KOREA

Arab–Israeli wars
In these frequent Middle East conflicts, the USA increasingly supported Israel while the USSR supported the Arab states.

Afghanistan
The Soviet invasion of Afghanistan in 1979, to support its communist government, caused a breakdown in relations between the USA and USSR.

SOMALIA

VIETNAM

CAMBODIA

MALAYA

Nehru of India
Prime Minister Nehru was one of the main leaders of the Non-Aligned Movement, whose members took neither side in the Cold War.

ETHIOPIA

Somalia
After Somalia invaded Ethiopia, in 1977, the USSR supported Ethiopia while the USA supported the Somalis.

Indian Ocean

Civil war in Angola
After 1975, Cuban- and Soviet-backed forces fought US- and South African-backed forces for control of the country.

ANGOLA

Malaya
In 1948 communist forces attacked European settlers in the Malay peninsula. Twelve years of jungle warfare followed, before British troops crushed the communist units in 1960.

Cambodia
In 1970 US planes secretly bombed Cambodia to prevent supplies reaching communists in South Vietnam. This dragged Cambodia into a decade of warfare.

AUSTRALIA

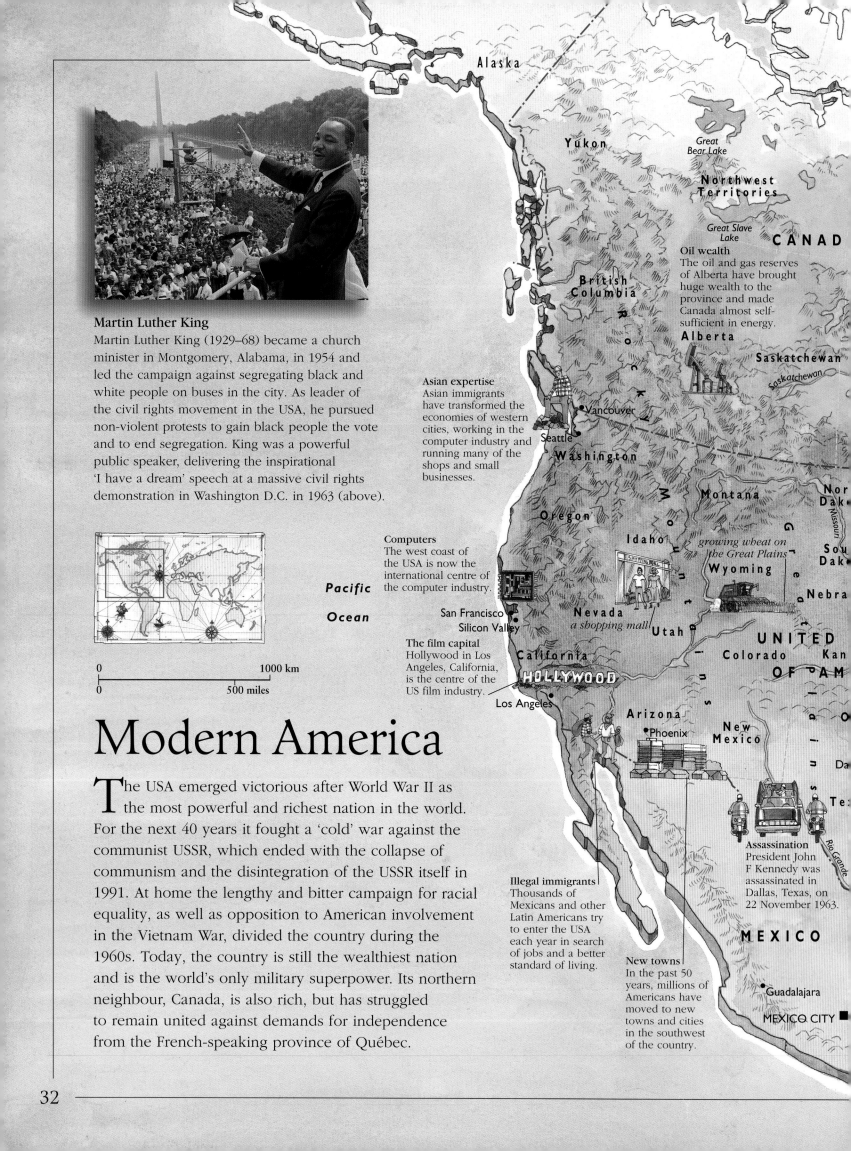

Martin Luther King

Martin Luther King (1929–68) became a church minister in Montgomery, Alabama, in 1954 and led the campaign against segregating black and white people on buses in the city. As leader of the civil rights movement in the USA, he pursued non-violent protests to gain black people the vote and to end segregation. King was a powerful public speaker, delivering the inspirational 'I have a dream' speech at a massive civil rights demonstration in Washington D.C. in 1963 (above).

0   1000 km
0   500 miles

Modern America

The USA emerged victorious after World War II as the most powerful and richest nation in the world. For the next 40 years it fought a 'cold' war against the communist USSR, which ended with the collapse of communism and the disintegration of the USSR itself in 1991. At home the lengthy and bitter campaign for racial equality, as well as opposition to American involvement in the Vietnam War, divided the country during the 1960s. Today, the country is still the wealthiest nation and is the world's only military superpower. Its northern neighbour, Canada, is also rich, but has struggled to remain united against demands for independence from the French-speaking province of Québec.

Asian expertise
Asian immigrants have transformed the economies of western cities, working in the computer industry and running many of the shops and small businesses.

Computers
The west coast of the USA is now the international centre of the computer industry.

Pacific

Ocean

The film capital
Hollywood in Los Angeles, California, is the centre of the US film industry.

Oil wealth
The oil and gas reserves of Alberta have brought huge wealth to the province and made Canada almost self-sufficient in energy.

Illegal immigrants
Thousands of Mexicans and other Latin Americans try to enter the USA each year in search of jobs and a better standard of living.

New towns
In the past 50 years, millions of Americans have moved to new towns and cities in the southwest of the country.

Assassination
President John F Kennedy was assassinated in Dallas, Texas, on 22 November 1963.

Alaska

Yukon

Great Bear Lake

Northwest Territories

Great Slave Lake

CANAD

Alberta

Saskatchewan

Saskatchewan

British Columbia

•Vancouver

Seattle

Washington

Oregon

Montana

Nor Dak

growing wheat on the Great Plains

Wyoming

Sou Dak

Idaho

Nevada

a shopping mall

Utah

Nebra

San Francisco
Silicon Valley

California

HOLLYWOOD

Los Angeles

Arizona

•Phoenix

New Mexico

Colorado

UNITED

Kan

OF AM

Da

Te

Rio Grande

MEXICO

•Guadalajara

MEXICO CITY ■

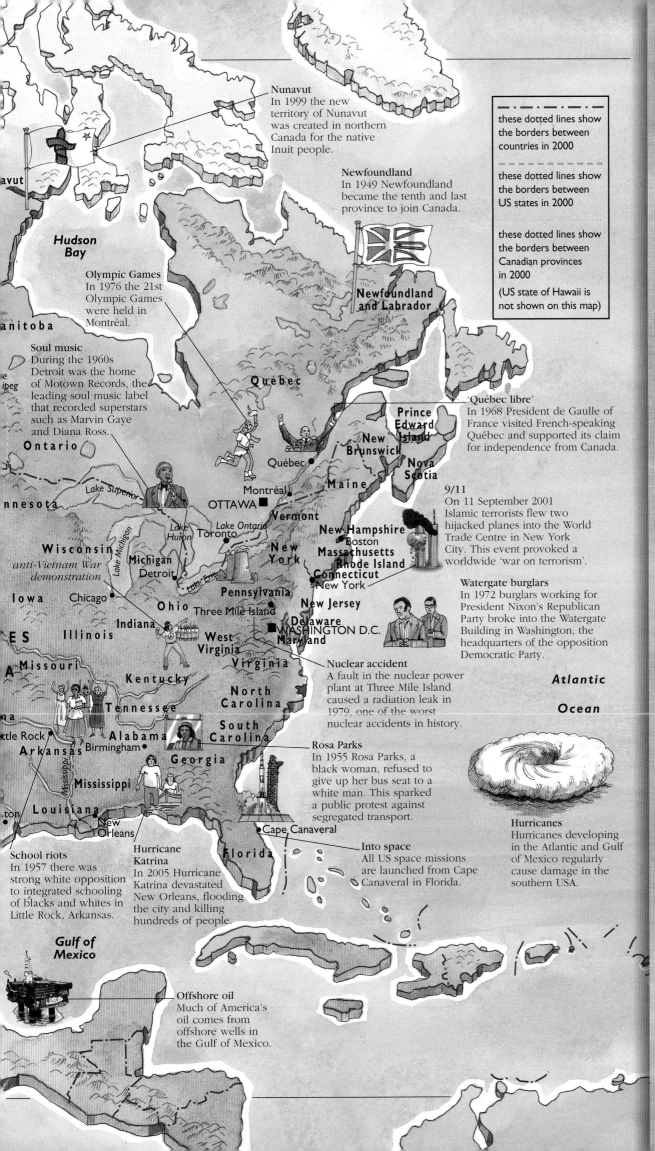

Nunavut
In 1999 the new territory of Nunavut was created in northern Canada for the native Inuit people.

Newfoundland
In 1949 Newfoundland became the tenth and last province to join Canada.

Hudson Bay

Olympic Games
In 1976 the 21st Olympic Games were held in Montréal.

these dotted lines show the borders between countries in 2000

these dotted lines show the borders between US states in 2000

these dotted lines show the borders between Canadian provinces in 2000

(US state of Hawaii is not shown on this map)

Newfoundland and Labrador

Soul music
During the 1960s Detroit was the home of Motown Records, the leading soul music label that recorded superstars such as Marvin Gaye and Diana Ross.

Québec

'Québec libre'
In 1968 President de Gaulle of France visited French-speaking Québec and supported its claim for independence from Canada.

Prince Edward Island
New Brunswick
Nova Scotia
Québec
Maine
Montréal
OTTAWA ■

9/11
On 11 September 2001 Islamic terrorists flew two hijacked planes into the World Trade Centre in New York City. This event provoked a worldwide 'war on terrorism'.

Vermont
New Hampshire
Boston
Massachusetts
Rhode Island
Connecticut

Lake Superior
Lake Huron
Lake Ontario
Lake Michigan
Lake Erie
Toronto

Wisconsin
anti-Vietnam War demonstration
Michigan
Detroit
New York
New York

Watergate burglars
In 1972 burglars working for President Nixon's Republican Party broke into the Watergate Building in Washington, the headquarters of the opposition Democratic Party.

Iowa
Chicago
Ohio
Three Mile Island
Pennsylvania
New Jersey
Delaware
■WASHINGTON D.C.
Maryland

Illinois
Indiana
West Virginia
Virginia

Nuclear accident
A fault in the nuclear power plant at Three Mile Island caused a radiation leak in 1979, one of the worst nuclear accidents in history.

Atlantic Ocean

Missouri
Kentucky
Tennessee
North Carolina

ttle Rock
Arkansas
Birmingham
Alabama
South Carolina
Georgia

Rosa Parks
In 1955 Rosa Parks, a black woman, refused to give up her bus seat to a white man. This sparked a public protest against segregated transport.

Mississippi
Mississippi
Louisiana
New Orleans

Hurricanes
Hurricanes developing in the Atlantic and Gulf of Mexico regularly cause damage in the southern USA.

School riots
In 1957 there was strong white opposition to integrated schooling of blacks and whites in Little Rock, Arkansas.

Hurricane Katrina
In 2005 Hurricane Katrina devastated New Orleans, flooding the city and killing hundreds of people.

Florida
Cape Canaveral

Into space
All US space missions are launched from Cape Canaveral in Florida.

Gulf of Mexico

Offshore oil
Much of America's oil comes from offshore wells in the Gulf of Mexico.

1940–today

1940

1945 President Roosevelt dies in office; Harry Truman takes over the presidency
1945 USA and its allies defeat Japan and Germany in World War II
1946 United Nations (UN) organization meets for the first time in New York City
1948 US armed services end racial segregation
1949 USA sets up North Atlantic Treaty Organization (NATO) to defend western Europe against communist aggression
1949 Newfoundland joins Canada

1950

1950 Senator Joe McCarthy starts an anti-communist witch-hunt
1950–53 US troops fight in Korea
1952 Wartime general Dwight D Eisenhower becomes president of the USA
1954 Supreme Court bans segregated education
1955 Montgomery bus boycott (protest) eventually ends segregated transport
1957 Federal troops help to integrate schools in Arkansas, so that black and white students can be educated together

1960

1960 John F Kennedy is elected as US president
1963 Martin Luther King leads massive civil rights march on Washington D.C.
1963 President Kennedy is assassinated
1964 Civil Rights Act bans racial discrimination
1965 USA sends many troops to Vietnam
1965 Race riots break out in US cities
1968 Martin Luther King is assassinated in Memphis, Tennessee
1968 Richard Nixon is elected as US president
1969 USA lands first astronauts on the Moon

1970

1972 Watergate break-in
1973 USA signs a ceasefire agreement with the North Vietnamese
1974 President Nixon is forced to resign over the Watergate affair

1976 Montréal hosts the Olympic Games
1976 Jimmy Carter is elected as US president

1979 Serious nuclear accident at Three Mile Island

1980

1980 Ronald Reagan is elected as US president
1980 In a referendum (public vote) Québec narrowly rejects independence from Canada
1981 Reagan survives assassination attempt

1985 USA and USSR begin talks to end the Cold War

1987 First limits on nuclear weapons agreed between the USA and the USSR
1988 George Bush is elected as US president

1990

1991 US troops lead a campaign to end Iraqi occupation of Kuwait in the Middle East
1992 Bill Clinton is elected as US president
1994 North American Free Trade Agreement between Canada, the USA and Mexico
1995 Québec again rejects independence from Canada in a second referendum

1998 Opponents try but fail to remove President Clinton from office
1999 Nunavut territory created in northern Canada

2000

2000 George W Bush is elected as US president
2001 9/11 (11 September) terrorist attacks in New York and Washington D.C.
2001 US-led invasion of Afghanistan, in response to 9/11, marks the start of the USA's 'war on terrorism'

2003 USA and its allies invade Iraq

2005 Hurricane Katrina devastates New Orleans

2010

China in the 20th century

In 1911 the Qing (Manchu) dynasty was overthrown and a republic was established. This led to a lengthy period of civil war and weak government in China. Nationalists, communists and, after 1937, invading Japanese forces all struggled for control of the country. Order was restored when the communists, under Mao Zedong, took power in 1949. They managed to unite the country, although their dictatorial policies caused huge social and economic upheaval. After the death of Mao in 1976, China began to adopt western economic policies, leading to an economic boom that has made the country one of the richest and most powerful nations in the world today.

Muslim China
The Uyghurs of the Xinjiang province are Turkic-speaking Muslims. They have more in common with their neighbours in central Asia than with the rest of China.

Xinjiang

0   1000 km

0   500 miles

The main food
Rice remains the staple diet for most Chinese people. Here a rice paddy (field) is being prepared for planting.

Population control
To restrict rapid population growth, a limit of 'one child per family' was set in 1979. Despite this, the Chinese population today totals 1.32 billion.

MONGOLIA

CHINA

The 'Great Leap Forward'
In 1958 Mao tried to create a true communist society by setting up huge agricultural communes, in which hundreds of peasant farmers would work. The project was a massive failure.

Traditional sports
Despite the rapid modernization and industrialization of China, traditional activities such as kite-flying are still very popular.

Tibet

Lhasa •

NEPAL

INDIA

Tibet
Governed by the Dalai Lama from the Potala Palace in Lhasa, Tibet was independent from 1913 until 1950, when Chinese communists occupied the country. A revolt in 1959 failed to regain independence.

INDIA

BANGLADESH

MYANMAR

Communist China
After they took power in 1949, the communists used posters, leaflets, banners and wall paintings to inspire the people to work harder towards achieving a communist society. This poster from 1965 bore the slogan 'Socialism advances in victory everywhere'. However, their methods were brutal and not always successful. The Great Leap Forward of 1958–61 aimed to set up massive farming communes, but it failed and millions died of hunger. The Cultural Revolution of 1966–76 aimed to stamp out old or traditional values, so that people could concentrate on revolution. It caused massive social and political disruption.

Communist China
On 1 October 1949, in Beijing, Chairman Mao formally introduced communist China under its new title, the Chinese People's Republic.

Railways
Russia built railways through Manchuria to reach ice-free ports in the Yellow Sea and Sea of Japan.

Manchuria
In 1931 Japan invaded the northern province of Manchuria and installed the last Chinese emperor, Pu-yi, as ruler.

Manchuria

The Olympics
Beijing will host the 29th modern Olympic Games in the summer of 2008.

Tiananmen Square
Chinese soldiers massacred pro-democracy demonstrators in Beijing's Tiananmen Square in June 1989.

Jehol

Sea of Japan

JAPAN

■ BEIJING

NORTH KOREA

SOUTH KOREA

The Last Emperor
Pu-yi was only six years old when he gave up his throne, in 1912, during the Chinese Revolution.

Yellow River

Yellow Sea

×Xuzhou

The Boxer Rebellion
In 1900–01 resentment towards foreign interference in China led to anti-western riots in northern cities such as the capital, Beijing.

The Battle of Xuzhou
The decisive victory of the communists over the nationalists, in the civil war, took place in Xuzhou in December 1948–January 1949.

Nanjing ●   Shanghai ●

Building boom
In recent years, new high-rise buildings have transformed the skyline of Shanghai and other major cities in the region.

East China Sea

Yangtze

The Long March
In 1934–35 100,000 communists trekked west and then north, for more than 8,000km, to escape the nationalist armies.

TAIWAN

Nationalist Taiwan
After the Chinese Civil War, the losing nationalists fled to the offshore island of Taiwan, which they still rule to this day.

Industrial success
Over the past 25 years, China has emerged as one of the world's biggest economies. It has produced a wide range of manufactured goods more cheaply than most competitors.

Guangzhou ●
Macao ●
Hong Kong ●
Hong Kong

The Europeans leave
In 1997 the British left their colony of Hong Kong. The Portuguese then left Macao in 1999. These were the last two European colonies in Asia.

LAOS

Hainan

South China Sea

VIETNAM

THAILAND

1900–today

1900
1900–01 Anti-western riots across northern China

1908 Pu-yi becomes last Qing (Manchu) emperor of China, aged two

1910
1911 Nationalists led by Sun Yat-sen overthrow Qing dynasty and establish a republic
1912 Emperor Pu-yi abdicates
1913 Tibet becomes independent

1917 China falls under the power of local warlords

1920
1921 Chinese Communist Party founded

1926 Chiang Kai-shek becomes the nationalist leader

1930
1931 Japanese invade Manchuria
1933 Japanese take province of Jehol
1934–35 The Long March
1937 Japanese launch full-scale invasion of China; more than 250,000 Chinese civilians are killed as Japanese overrun the nationalist capital, Nanjing

1940
1945 After victory over the Japanese, civil war begins in China between the nationalists and the communists

1949 Mao Zedong proclaims the Chinese People's Republic in Beijing; nationalists flee to Taiwan
1950
1950 Chinese occupy Tibet

1958–61 The 'Great Leap Forward' fails to achieve a true communist society
1959 Tibetan rebellions fail to remove the Chinese
1960
1960 China falls out with the USSR
1964 China explodes its first atomic weapon
1965–68 Cultural Revolution: Mao urges the Chinese youth to reject the Soviet style of communism; schools are closed, and the movement turns violent as teachers, intellectuals and others are persecuted

1970
1972 US president Nixon visits China

1976 Chairman Mao (Mao Zedong) dies

1979 'One child per family' policy introduced in China

1980
1980 Deng Xiaoping becomes leader and begins economic reforms
1984 Major reforms introduced to modernize Chinese industry

1989 Pro-democracy movement crushed in Beijing
1990

1992 China begins to introduce a 'socialist market economy'

1997 British return Hong Kong to China

1999 Portuguese return Macao to China
2000

2007 China becomes the world's third richest nation, after the USA and Japan
2008 Beijing hosts the summer Olympic Games

2010

UNITED STATES OF AMERICA

WASHINGTON D.C.

Mexican Revolution
Revolutionary armies led by Emiliano Zapata and 'Pancho' Villa contributed to the lawlessness that gripped Mexico from 1910–24.

MEXICO

Guadalajara

MEXICO CITY

Gulf of Mexico

Cause of war
The unexplained sinking of the *USS Maine* in Havana Harbour, Cuba, was the main cause of war between the USA and Spain in 1898. The outcome of the war was the independence of Cuba.

The Rough Riders
Future US president Theodore Roosevelt led a group of volunteers – the 'Rough Riders' – to fight against Spain in the 1898 war.

Fidel Castro
In 1959 Fidel Castro seized power in Cuba and turned the country into a communist state. He still holds power today.

NASSAU
BAHAMAS

HAVANA
CUBA
San Juan

HAITI
PORT-AU-PRINCE

DOMINICAN REPUBLIC
SANTO DOMINGO

Puerto Rico

KINGSTON
JAMAICA

Caribbean Sea

Atlantic Ocean

Sugar
In 1815 sugar plantations covered more than 90 per cent of Barbados to satisfy British demand for the much-needed crop.

BARBADOS

freed slaves in the West Indies, 1834

W e s t   I n d i e s

Colonies
Today, French Guiana is the only European colony on the American mainland – although France, Britain and the Netherlands also own some islands in the Caribbean.

GEORGETOWN
GUYANA

PARAMARIBO
SURINAME

Kourou
FRENCH GUIANA

Imperial Brazil
In 1822 Pedro, Portuguese regent of Brazil, declared independence from Portugal and became emperor of Brazil. His son, Pedro II, ruled the country until a republic was declared in 1889.

Pedro II, emperor of Brazil

BRAZIL

CARACAS
VENEZUELA

Oil
The oil deposits of Lake Maracaibo are among the largest outside the Middle East. This has made Venezuela a very wealthy country.

BOGOTÁ
COLOMBIA

Cocaine
In recent years Colombia has become the world's main supplier of the illegal drug cocaine.

a Colombian coca plant

QUITO
ECUADOR

Amazon

Amazonia

a rubber tree being tapped

Rubber
During the 1890s the Amazon basin became one of the world's major producers of rubber.

PERU

Andes

Simón Bolívar
Bolívar achieved the independence of Venezuela, Colombia and Ecuador from Spanish rule after 1819. He is the only man to have a country, Bolivia, named after him today.

José de San Martín
José de San Martín liberated Argentina and Peru from Spanish rule in 1816–21.

PANAMA
PANAMA CITY

Panama Canal

The Panama Canal
In 1904 US engineers began to build a canal across Panama, linking the Pacific Ocean and the Caribbean Sea. It was opened for shipping in 1914.

COSTA RICA
SAN JOSÉ

NICARAGUA
MANAGUA

HONDURAS
TEGUCIGALPA

BELMOPAN
BELIZE

GUATEMALA
GUATEMALA CITY

SAN SALVADOR
EL SALVADOR

One-crop countries
During the late 1880s, many Central American countries became dependent on one crop for their income – mainly coffee or bananas.

Pacific Ocean

_ . _ . _ . _   these dotted lines show the borders between countries in 2000

2000 km

1000 miles

0

0

Latin America

Charismatic liberators such as Simón Bolívar helped Latin America to win independence from Spain in the early 1800s. The empire of Brazil also gained its independence from Portugal before becoming a republic. All these new nations were politically unstable and were often governed by dictators. During the 20th century, social divisions between rich and poor led to long periods of military rule and revolutionary upheaval. The USA supported the continent's independence from European rule, but often treated Central American nations as its backyard, controlling their economies and intervening when their elected governments threatened US interests.

The end of slavery

The trade in African slaves across the Atlantic, to work in the plantations of Central and South America, was ended by Britain in 1807 and France in 1815 – but a variety of traders continued to supply slaves to Brazil and Cuba until the 1860s. The institution of slavery itself was abolished in all British colonies in 1834, but survived in Brazil until 1888. A lack of alternative work, however, meant that many former slaves were forced to continue working on the plantations as paid labourers.

BRASÍLIA

Rio de Janeiro

Brasília
The capital of Brazil was moved from the overcrowded Rio de Janeiro to the new, inland city of Brasília in 1960.

São Paulo

Oil war
The lure of oil in the Gran Chaco region caused war between Bolivia and Paraguay in 1932–35, although no oil was ever found there.

Immigration
From the mid-1850s, more than 4.5 million immigrants from southern Europe arrived in Argentina. This was followed by 115,000 Jews fleeing oppression in Russia after 1881.

The Falklands
In March 1982 Argentine forces invaded the British-owned Falkland Islands. Three months later they were defeated by British forces.

Falkland Islands

Gauchos
Cowboys known as gauchos tended the huge cattle ranches in the pampas regions of northern Argentina and Uruguay.

Evita
Juan Perón and his wife Eva (Evita) became hugely popular leaders in Argentina after 1946.

Che Guevara
The revolutionary leader Che Guevara was killed in Bolivia in 1967 while trying to encourage the tin miners to revolt.

PARAGUAY

Gran Chaco

ASUNCIÓN

URUGUAY

MONTEVIDEO

BUENOS AIRES

BOLIVIA

LA PAZ

Andes

CHILE

ARGENTINA

SANTIAGO

Ayacucho

Pacific Ocean

Bernardo O'Higgins
The liberator of Chile was the son of an Irishman who spent his childhood in Europe. He returned to Chile to lead the independence struggle after 1813.

Allende
In 1973 a US-backed military coup overthrew President Salvador Allende of Chile, the world's first democratically elected Marxist head of state.

1800–2000

1800
1804 Haiti becomes independent of France
1807 Britain ends dealings in slave trade
1811 Paraguay independent of Spain
1819–22 Simón Bolívar wins independence for Greater Colombia
1821 Mexico and Central America win independence from Spain
1823 USA proclaims the Monroe Doctrine, warning European powers not to intervene again in Latin America

1825
1825 Bolivia independent of Spain
1828 Uruguay independent of Brazil
1830 Venezuela and Ecuador gain independence from Colombia
1830s Mass immigration from southern Europe to Brazil
1831 Pedro II becomes emperor of Brazil
1834 Britain frees its West Indian slaves
1846–48 Mexico loses its northern territories in war with the USA

1850
1850s Mass immigration from southern Europe to Argentina

1864–70 War of the Triple Alliance between Paraguay and its neighbours

1875
1879–83 War of the Pacific: Chile defeats Peru; Bolivia loses access to the sea
1881 Jews flee persecution in Russia and settle in Argentina
1888 Pedro II abolishes slavery in Brazil
1889 Pedro II overthrown; Brazil becomes a republic
1898 Spanish-American War: Cuba gains independence from Spain; the USA gains Puerto Rico

1900
1903 USA helps Panama to gain independence from Colombia

1910–24 Mexican Revolution: the USA intervenes to restore order
1912–34 US troops police Nicaragua
1914 Panama Canal opens

1917 USA gains the Virgin Islands from Denmark

1925

1932–35 Gran Chaco war between Bolivia and Paraguay
1937–45 Fascist dictatorship runs Brazil
1940–42 Ecuador and Peru fight over territories in Amazonia
1946 Juan Perón becomes president of Argentina

1950

1959 Fidel Castro seizes power in Cuba
1962 Trinidad and Jamaica win independence from Britain
1964–85 Army governs Brazil
1966–83 Most British colonies gain independence

1973 President Allende of Chile toppled by a US-backed military coup

1975
1975 Dutch give independence to Suriname
1976–82 'Dirty war' between the Argentine military and guerilla forces
1984–90 USA supports the Contras against the Nicaraguan government
1988 Mexico joins Canada and the USA in the North American Free Trade Agreement
1989 Democracy returns to Chile
1998 Hugo Chávez is elected as president of Venezuela and frequently clashes with the USA

2000

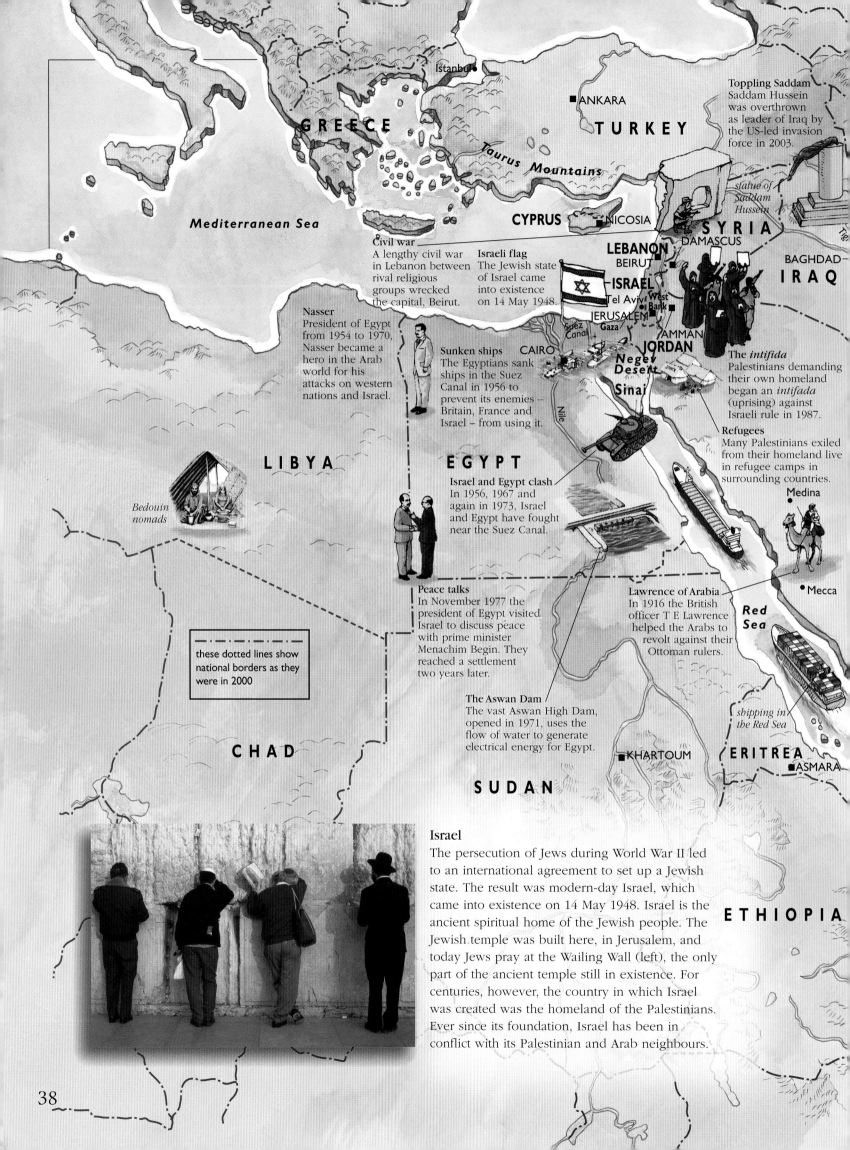

ANKARA

GREECE

TURKEY

Istanbul

Taurus Mountains

Mediterranean Sea

CYPRUS ■NICOSIA

Toppling Saddam
Saddam Hussein was overthrown as leader of Iraq by the US-led invasion force in 2003.

statue of Saddam Hussein

SYRIA
DAMASCUS

LEBANON
BEIRUT ■

ISRAEL
Tel Aviv ■
West Bank
JERUSALEM
Gaza

BAGHDAD
IRAQ

Civil war
A lengthy civil war in Lebanon between rival religious groups wrecked the capital, Beirut.

Israeli flag
The Jewish state of Israel came into existence on 14 May 1948.

Nasser
President of Egypt from 1954 to 1970, Nasser became a hero in the Arab world for his attacks on western nations and Israel.

Sunken ships
The Egyptians sank ships in the Suez Canal in 1956 to prevent its enemies – Britain, France and Israel – from using it.

CAIRO

Suez Canal

JORDAN
AMMAN

Negev Desert

Sinai

Nile

The intifida
Palestinians demanding their own homeland began an *intifada* (uprising) against Israeli rule in 1987.

Refugees
Many Palestinians exiled from their homeland live in refugee camps in surrounding countries.

Medina

LIBYA

Bedouin nomads

EGYPT

Israel and Egypt clash
In 1956, 1967 and again in 1973, Israel and Egypt have fought near the Suez Canal.

• Mecca

Lawrence of Arabia
In 1916 the British officer T E Lawrence helped the Arabs to revolt against their Ottoman rulers.

Red Sea

Peace talks
In November 1977 the president of Egypt visited Israel to discuss peace with prime minister Menachim Begin. They reached a settlement two years later.

these dotted lines show national borders as they were in 2000

The Aswan Dam
The vast Aswan High Dam, opened in 1971, uses the flow of water to generate electrical energy for Egypt.

shipping in the Red Sea

CHAD

■KHARTOUM

ERITREA
■ASMARA

SUDAN

Israel

The persecution of Jews during World War II led to an international agreement to set up a Jewish state. The result was modern-day Israel, which came into existence on 14 May 1948. Israel is the ancient spiritual home of the Jewish people. The Jewish temple was built here, in Jerusalem, and today Jews pray at the Wailing Wall (left), the only part of the ancient temple still in existence. For centuries, however, the country in which Israel was created was the homeland of the Palestinians. Ever since its foundation, Israel has been in conflict with its Palestinian and Arab neighbours.

ETHIOPIA

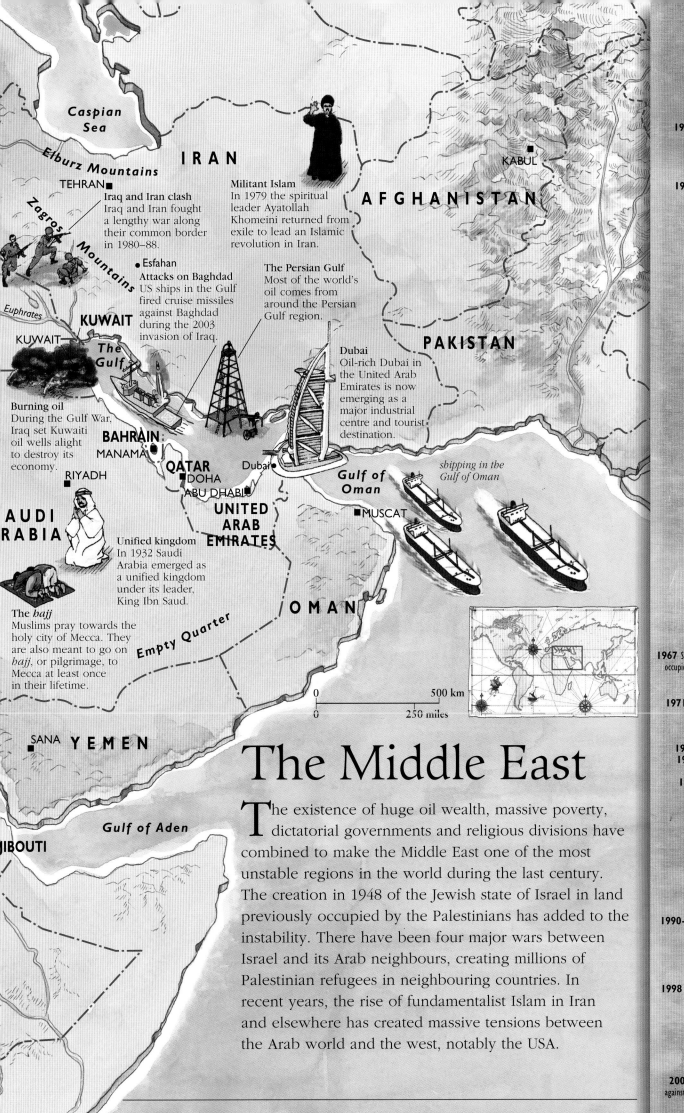

Caspian Sea

Elburz Mountains

TEHRAN■

IRAN

Zagros Mountains

Iraq and Iran clash
Iraq and Iran fought a lengthy war along their common border in 1980–88.

Euphrates

● Esfahan

Attacks on Baghdad
US ships in the Gulf fired cruise missiles against Baghdad during the 2003 invasion of Iraq.

Militant Islam
In 1979 the spiritual leader Ayatollah Khomeini returned from exile to lead an Islamic revolution in Iran.

The Persian Gulf
Most of the world's oil comes from around the Persian Gulf region.

KABUL ■

AFGHANISTAN

PAKISTAN

Dubai
Oil-rich Dubai in the United Arab Emirates is now emerging as a major industrial centre and tourist destination.

KUWAIT

KUWAIT─

The Gulf

Burning oil
During the Gulf War, Iraq set Kuwaiti oil wells alight to destroy its economy.

● RIYADH

BAHRAIN
MANAMA ■

QATAR
■DOHA

ABU DHABI■

Dubai ●

UNITED ARAB EMIRATES

■MUSCAT

Gulf of Oman

shipping in the Gulf of Oman

AUDI RABIA

Unified kingdom
In 1932 Saudi Arabia emerged as a unified kingdom under its leader, King Ibn Saud.

The *hajj*
Muslims pray towards the holy city of Mecca. They are also meant to go on *hajj*, or pilgrimage, to Mecca at least once in their lifetime.

Empty Quarter

OMAN

0 ———— 500 km
0 ———— 250 miles

SANA ■ YEMEN

Gulf of Aden

IBOUTI

The Middle East

The existence of huge oil wealth, massive poverty, dictatorial governments and religious divisions have combined to make the Middle East one of the most unstable regions in the world during the last century. The creation in 1948 of the Jewish state of Israel in land previously occupied by the Palestinians has added to the instability. There have been four major wars between Israel and its Arab neighbours, creating millions of Palestinian refugees in neighbouring countries. In recent years, the rise of fundamentalist Islam in Iran and elsewhere has created massive tensions between the Arab world and the west, notably the USA.

1910–today

1910
1914 Ottoman Turks control most of the region

1916 Arabs revolt against Ottoman rule
1917 Britain issues the Balfour Declaration, promising Jews a homeland in Palestine
1918 Ottoman empire collapses at the end of World War I
1920
1920 Britain takes over Palestine and Iraq; France takes over Syria and Lebanon
1922 Egypt gains independence from Britain

1930
1932 Kingdom of Saudi Arabia founded
1932 Iraq gains independence from Britain

1938 Saudi Arabia begins to export oil

1940

1946 Jordan gains independence from Britain
1946 Syria and Lebanon gain full independence from France
1948 Israel founded; first war between Israel and its Arab neighbours
1950

1952 Political coup in Egypt overthrows the king
1954 Nasser becomes president of Egypt
1956 Israel invades Egypt in association with Britain and France

1960
1961 Kuwait gains independence

1964 Palestinian Liberation Organization (PLO) founded

1967 Six-Day War: Israel defeats Arab armies and occupies the West Bank, Gaza and Golan Heights
1970
1971 Britain withdraws from the Persian Gulf: the United Arab Emirates are formed
1973 Egypt and Syria attack Israel
1975–89 Civil war in Lebanon
1977 Peace talks between Egypt and Israel
1979 Egypt and Israel sign a peace treaty
1979 Islamic revolution in Iran
1979 Saddam Hussein is president of Iraq
1980
1980–88 Iran-Iraq War caused by Iraqi invasion of neighbouring Iran
1982–2000 Israel invades and occupies southern Lebanon

1987 Palestinians begin an 'intifada' (uprising) against Israel

1990
1990 Unification of Yemen
1990–91 Gulf War: Iraq invades Kuwait but is expelled after international intervention
1993 Israel recognizes the PLO as representatives of the Palestinians

1998 First limited rule for Palestinians in Israel
2000
2003 US-led force invades and occupies Iraq, and overthrows Saddam Hussein
2004 Revolt begins in Iraq against the occupation of US and allied troops
2005 Israel withdraws from Gaza, handing it over to the Palestinians
2006 Saddam Hussein found guilty of 'crimes against humanity' and executed on 30 December
2010

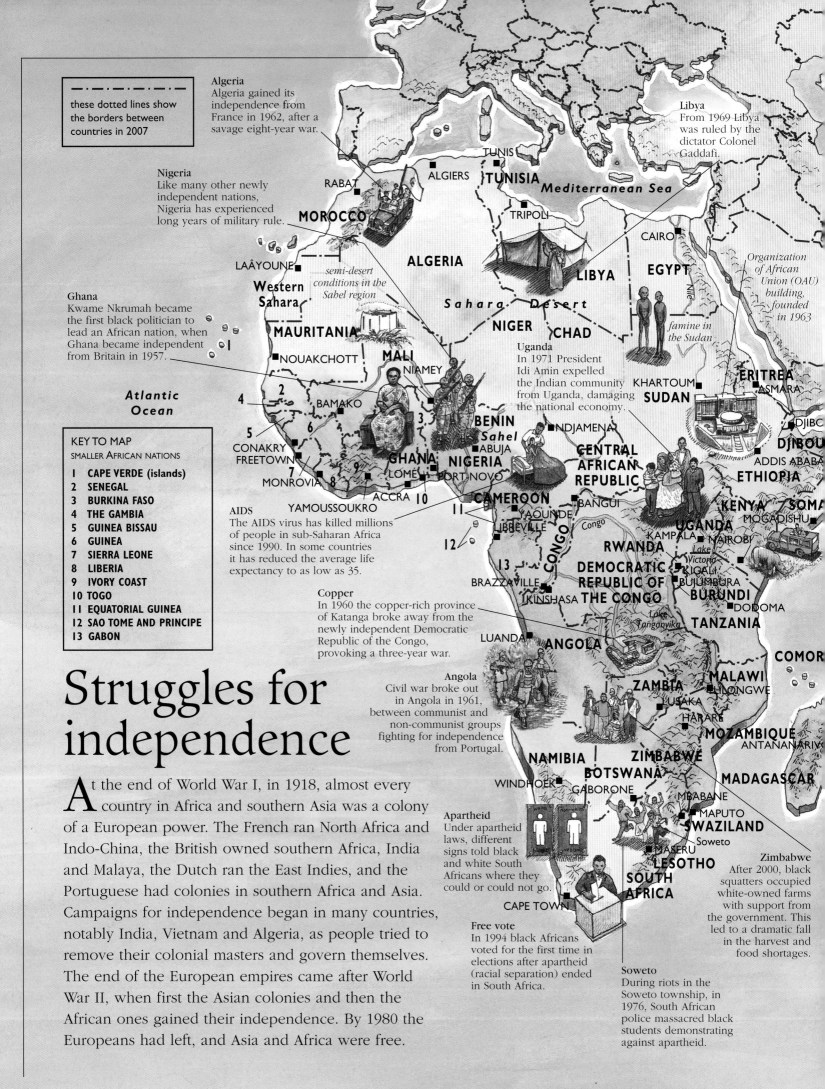

these dotted lines show the borders between countries in 2007

Algeria
Algeria gained its independence from France in 1962, after a savage eight-year war.

Libya
From 1969 Libya was ruled by the dictator Colonel Gaddafi.

Nigeria
Like many other newly independent nations, Nigeria has experienced long years of military rule.

Ghana
Kwame Nkrumah became the first black politician to lead an African nation, when Ghana became independent from Britain in 1957.

Organization of African Union (OAU) building, founded in 1963

famine in the Sudan

Uganda
In 1971 President Idi Amin expelled the Indian community from Uganda, damaging the national economy.

AIDS
The AIDS virus has killed millions of people in sub-Saharan Africa since 1990. In some countries it has reduced the average life expectancy to as low as 35.

Copper
In 1960 the copper-rich province of Katanga broke away from the newly independent Democratic Republic of the Congo, provoking a three-year war.

Angola
Civil war broke out in Angola in 1961, between communist and non-communist groups fighting for independence from Portugal.

Apartheid
Under apartheid laws, different signs told black and white South Africans where they could or could not go.

Free vote
In 1994 black Africans voted for the first time in elections after apartheid (racial separation) ended in South Africa.

Soweto
During riots in the Soweto township, in 1976, South African police massacred black students demonstrating against apartheid.

Zimbabwe
After 2000, black squatters occupied white-owned farms with support from the government. This led to a dramatic fall in the harvest and food shortages.

Atlantic Ocean

Mediterranean Sea

KEY TO MAP
SMALLER AFRICAN NATIONS

1 CAPE VERDE (islands)
2 SENEGAL
3 BURKINA FASO
4 THE GAMBIA
5 GUINEA BISSAU
6 GUINEA
7 SIERRA LEONE
8 LIBERIA
9 IVORY COAST
10 TOGO
11 EQUATORIAL GUINEA
12 SAO TOME AND PRINCIPE
13 GABON

Map labels:
RABAT, ALGIERS, TUNIS, TUNISIA, TRIPOLI, CAIRO, MOROCCO, LAÂYOUNE, Western Sahara, ALGERIA, LIBYA, EGYPT, MAURITANIA, NOUAKCHOTT, semi-desert conditions in the Sahel region, Sahara Desert, NIGER, CHAD, NDJAMENA, MALI, NIAMEY, BAMAKO, BENIN, Sahel, ABUJA, GHANA, NIGERIA, LOMÉ, PORT-NOVO, CENTRAL AFRICAN REPUBLIC, KHARTOUM, SUDAN, ERITREA, ASMARA, DJIBOUTI, ADDIS ABABA, ETHIOPIA, CONAKRY, FREETOWN, MONROVIA, ACCRA, YAMOUSSOUKRO, CAMEROON, YAOUNDE, LIBREVILLE, BANGUI, Congo, CONGO, UGANDA, KAMPALA, KENYA, NAIROBI, SOMALIA, MOGADISHU, RWANDA, KIGALI, DEMOCRATIC REPUBLIC OF THE CONGO, BUJUMBURA, BURUNDI, DODOMA, Lake Victoria, Lake Tanganyika, TANZANIA, BRAZZAVILLE, KINSHASA, LUANDA, ANGOLA, COMOROS, ZAMBIA, LUSAKA, MALAWI, LILONGWE, HARARE, MOZAMBIQUE, ANTANANARIVO, NAMIBIA, ZIMBABWE, BOTSWANA, WINDHOEK, GABORONE, MBABANE, MAPUTO, SWAZILAND, MADAGASCAR, Soweto, MASERU, LESOTHO, SOUTH AFRICA, CAPE TOWN

Struggles for independence

A t the end of World War I, in 1918, almost every country in Africa and southern Asia was a colony of a European power. The French ran North Africa and Indo-China, the British owned southern Africa, India and Malaya, the Dutch ran the East Indies, and the Portuguese had colonies in southern Africa and Asia. Campaigns for independence began in many countries, notably India, Vietnam and Algeria, as people tried to remove their colonial masters and govern themselves. The end of the European empires came after World War II, when first the Asian colonies and then the African ones gained their independence. By 1980 the Europeans had left, and Asia and Africa were free.

Kashmir
Ever since their independence in 1947, Pakistan and India have frequently fought over the state of Kashmir.

ISLAMABAD

Amritsar
The killing of 379 Indians by British troops in 1919 increased support for Indian independence from Britain.

Kashmir

Himalayas

Quetta

Delhi

NEPAL

PAKISTAN

KATHMANDU

NEW DELHI

Indus

Karachi

Ganges

INDIA

THIMPHU

BHUTAN

DHAKA

Bangladesh
Bangladesh became independent from the rest of Pakistan in 1971. Its low-lying land is often flooded by the sea.

Cambodia
After 1975, a hard-line communist government murdered more than two million people in Cambodia, before it was expelled in 1979.

East China Sea

Vietnam
Communist soldiers fought first the French and then the Americans before Vietnam was finally united under their rule in 1975.

Kolkata (Calcutta)

Mumbai (Bombay)

BANGLADESH

MYANMAR (BURMA)

HANOI

LAOS

VIENTIANE

Partition
When India became independent in 1947, millions of Muslims fled for their lives into neighbouring Pakistan. The Hindus fled in the opposite direction.

Bay of Bengal

the Asian tsunami of 2004

YANGON (RANGOON)

VIETNAM

MANILA

Madras (Chennai)

Arabian Sea

Nehru
Pandit Nehru led India to independence and became its first prime minister. He led the country until his death in 1964.

the Petronas Towers in Kuala Lumpur, Malaysia

CAMBODIA

PHNOM PENH

South China Sea

logging in Indonesia

PHILIPPINES

SRI LANKA

Malaysia
Since independence in 1957, Malaysia has become one of the richest countries in the world, with many impressive, high-rise buildings.

Kuala Lumpur

MALAYSIA

SINGAPORE

INDONESIA

Tamil Tigers
Since 1983 the minority Tamils have fought a vicious civil war for independence from the majority Sinhalese people of Sri Lanka.

Singapore
The island of Singapore became independent from Malaysia in 1965, and has now developed as a major shipping port for the entire region.

JAKARTA

SEYCHELLES

Indian Ocean

East Timor
In 2002 the former Portuguese colony of East Timor finally gained its independence after Indonesia occupied the country in 1975.

MAURITIUS

0 ——— 3000 km
0 ——— 1500 miles

AUSTRALIA

Indian independence
The struggle for Indian independence from British rule was led by the Congress Party, among whose leaders was Mahatma Gandhi. In 1930 Gandhi led a symbolic march to the sea, where he picked up salt. This broke the British government's control over the production of salt and made British rule look stupid in the process. These and other peaceful protests eventually forced the British to leave India, which was partitioned in 1947 between Muslim Pakistan and the mainly Hindu India.

1918 World War I ends
1918 Most of Africa, southern and southeast Asia are under European colonial rule

1920 Britain, France and South Africa take over former German colonies in Africa
1922 Egypt gains independence from Britain

1926 Morocco revolts against French rule

1930
1935 Britain grants home rule to Indian provinces
1935–36 Italy invades Abyssinia (Ethiopia)
1940–41 Japan occupies French Indo-China
1941 Britain occupies Italian east African colonies and frees Abyssinia
1941 Ho Chi Minh forms nationalist Viet Minh guerilla group in Vietnam
1941–42 Japan occupies southeast Asia
1946 Philippines independent of the USA
1946–54 French fight Viet Minh for control of Vietnam
1947 Britain grants independence to India and Pakistan
1948 Britain grants independence to Burma and Ceylon (Sri Lanka)
1949 Dutch grant Indonesia independence

1950
1951 Libya becomes independent
1954 France leaves Indo-China; Laos and Cambodia become independent
1955 Sudan gains independence from joint British-Egyptian rule
1956 France grants independence to Morocco and Tunisia
1957 Britain grants Malaya independence
1957 Ghana becomes the first independent black African nation
1960–62 Most of sub-Saharan Africa gains independence
1962 France grants Algeria independence
1963 Federation of Malaysia created
1964–75 USA supports South Vietnam against communist North Vietnam
1965 Singapore independent of Malaysia

1970
1971 Bangladesh breaks away from Pakistan

1975 Indonesia occupies the Portuguese colony of East Timor
1975 Vietnam is reunited under communist rule
1975 Portuguese colonies in Africa win independence, but civil war continues in Angola
1975–79 Khmer Rouge military regime kills millions in Cambodia
1980 Zimbabwe, Britain's last remaining colony in Africa, wins independence
1983 Tamil Tiger guerillas begin their fight for independence in Sri Lanka

1990
1990 Namibia gains independence from South Africa
1993 Eritrea gains independence from Ethiopia
1994 Apartheid (racial segregation) comes to an end in South Africa; Nelson Mandela elected as president of South Africa
1994 Genocide (mass extermination of native people) in Rwanda by extremist militia groups
2002 East Timor gains independence from Indonesia
2002 Civil war ends in Angola after a ceasefire is arranged
2004 Tsunami devastates coastal regions around the Indian Ocean

2010

Modern Europe

In 1945, after the defeat of Germany at the end of World War II, Europe became divided into two parts. The communist east contained countries occupied by Soviet troops, while the capitalist west was home to democratic nations. This division of Europe – known as the Iron Curtain – lasted until 1990, when communism collapsed in the east and democratic governments took over. The USSR itself collapsed the following year and broke up into 15 separate nations. Since then, much of Europe has become more united within the European Union, although huge economic differences still exist between the poorer east and the wealthier west.

these dotted lines show the state borders in Europe in 2007

0   500 km
0   250 miles

KEY TO MAP
SMALLER EUROPEAN NATIONS

1 SLOVENIA
2 CROATIA
3 BOSNIA AND HERZEGOVINA
4 SERBIA
5 MONTENEGRO
6 MACEDONIA

The Berlin Wall
In 1989 the wall that divided communist East Berlin from capitalist West Berlin was pulled down. The city was reunited.

First female PM
In 1979 Margaret Thatcher became the first woman prime minister of Britain (also, officially, known as the United Kingdom).

The Nuremburg trials
Twenty-one leading Nazis were put on trial in 1946 for war crimes. Eleven of them were sentenced to death.

Shipping
Rotterdam is Europe's busiest port.

'The Troubles'
Irish republican opposition to British rule in Northern Ireland erupted into violence in 1969.

The Channel Tunnel
A rail tunnel link under the English Channel, between England and France, opened in 1994.

Fishing
Industrial fishing by European trawler fleets has seriously depleted fish stocks in recent years.

Farm power
Farmers have huge political and economic influence in modern-day France.

The May Uprising
In 1968 riots erupted between students and police in France.

Democracy triumphs
In 1981 Colonel Molina tried to end democracy in Spain by storming the parliament. He failed.

Package tours
Since the 1950s, mass tourism has brought great wealth to large parts of Spain.

European Union
In 1957 six countries signed the Treaty of Rome, setting up the European Economic Community (EEC).

Revolution of the Flowers
A military coup in Portugal in 1974 overthrew almost 50 years of dictatorship and brought democracy back to the country.

NORWAY
SWEDEN
OSLO
STOCKHOL
North Sea
DENMARK
COPENHAGEN
Northern Ireland
DUBLIN
IRELAND
UNITED KINGDOM
LONDON
AMSTERDAM
NETHERLANDS
BERLIN
BELGIUM
Rotterdam
GERMANY
BRUSSELS
PRAGUE
LUXEMBOURG
CZECH
LUXEMBOURG
PARIS
FRANCE
VIENN
AUSTRIA
BERN ALPS
SWITZERLAND
LJUBLJANA
ZAGR
English Channel
Pyrenees
Corsica
ITALY
ROME
SPAIN
MADRID
Atlantic Ocean
PORTUGAL
LISBON
Balearic Islands
Sardinia
Mediterranean Sea
Sicily
Malte

The European Union

France and Germany had gone to war with each other in 1870, 1914 and 1939. After 1945, they decided to live together in peace. In 1952 the two countries, along with Italy and the Benelux nations (Belgium, Luxembourg and the Netherlands), merged their coal and steel industries. The six then set up the European Economic Community (EEC) in 1957. Britain joined in 1973 and eight more nations by 1995. Today the European Union, as it is now called, has 27 members, a single currency, and its own parliament and laws.

FINLAND

Solidarity
The independent Solidarity trade union took on and defeated the communists in Poland in the 1980s.

HELSINKI ■

■ TALLINN
ESTONIA

■ MOSCOW

Reforming communism
Mikhail Gorbachev tried to reform the communist USSR after 1985, but he could not prevent its collapse in 1991.

LATVIA
RIGA ■

Seeking peace
In 1970 the West German chancellor Willy Brandt went to Warsaw, in Poland, to seek peace between eastern and western Europe.

RUSSIAN FEDERATION

LITHUANIA

Baltic Sea

SOLIDARNOŚĆ

VILNIUS ■

■ MINSK

BELARUS

Nuclear catastrophe
In 1986 a reactor exploded at the Chernobyl nuclear power plant, near Kiev. It remains the worst nuclear accident in history.

WARSAW ■

Chechnya
Russia invaded the break-away republic of Chechnya in 1994–96. The war has wrecked the Chechen capital, Grozny.

POLAND

■ KIEV

Ukraine
The Orange Revolution in Ukraine in 2004 overturned the results of a rigged presidential election and handed power to the democratic opposition.

Democracy
After the collapse of communism in 1989, voters across eastern Europe elected democratic governments.

UKRAINE

...LIC

SLOVAKIA
...ATISLAVA

MOLDOVA
CHISINAU ■

Chechnya

Caucasus

GEORGIA

■ BUDAPEST

HUNGARY

Romania
One of the worst communist dictators was Nicolae Ceausescu of Romania, who erected massive public buildings throughout the country.

Georgia
The Rose Revolution of 2004 introduced democracy to Georgia for the first time since its independence from the USSR in 1991.

ROMANIA
BUCHAREST ■

BELGRADE ■

3

4

Black Sea

BULGARIA

...RAJEVO ■

5

SOFIA ■

Oil supplies
In 2005 an oil pipeline was opened, taking oil from Baku on the Caspian Sea, through Georgia and Turkey, to Ceyhan on the Mediterranean coast.

PODGORICA ■

1

■ SKOPJE

6

● Istanbul

TIRANA ■
ALBANIA

TURKEY
ANKARA ■

The Olympics
The Olympic Games returned to their spiritual home in Greece when Athens hosted the games in 2004.

Ceyhan

Cyprus
UN (United Nations) troops keep Greeks and Turks apart on the divided island of Cyprus.

War in Bosnia
A vicious civil war from 1992–95 led to atrocities against ethnic minorities in Bosnia.

GREECE

■ ATHENS

■ NICOSIA
CYPRUS

Crete

Mediterranean Sea

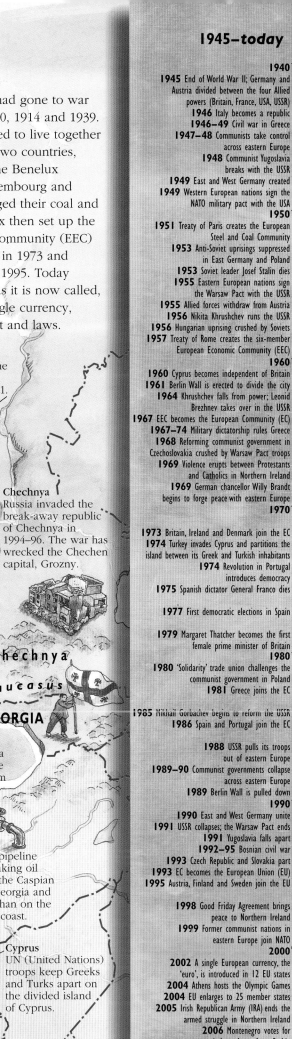

The world today:
Looking to the future

The world at the start of the new millennium is a remarkably challenging place. Rapid population growth – there are at least 6.4 billion people squashed onto the planet today – and industrial development are straining the world's resources and leading to environmental disasters. Millions of people have left their homes in search of wealth and happiness, creating social and economic problems in both the countries they have left and those where they have settled. Tensions exist between rich and poor, and between people of different religious faiths. But there are also many ways in which human beings are meeting these challenges, and trying to solve the many problems of the modern world.

Multiculturalism
In the past 50 years, large numbers of people left poverty and often oppression in poorer parts of the world and moved to the rich nations of Europe, North America and Australia in search of work and a better life. These migrants took with them their own religions and cultures, turning their host cities into vibrant multi-cultural, multi-ethnic places. While they have benefited economically, many migrants have faced racial hatred and social isolation in their new countries. This picture (above) shows children participating in the Free Time arts festival, held every summer in London, UK. The festival is led by artists from a wide variety of cultures.

A large percentage of the world's population now lives in heavily built-up urban environments. This is the sprawling city of Los Angeles in California, USA.

AIDS awareness

During the 1980s a new disease – AIDS, or Acquired Immune Deficiency Syndrome – spread around the world. There is no known cure for the disease, although an expensive combination of drugs can slow its progress. More than 40 million people now have AIDS, the vast majority of them living in Africa and Asia. Its effect on poorer nations is immense, reducing the overall life expectancy of the population and creating many thousands of orphaned or ill children, such as this one in Soweto, South Africa (left).

Charity groups working in Africa and Asia have set up projects to help children whose parents have died from AIDS.

Every year, World AIDS Day aims to raise awareness of the disease and raise money for sufferers. Here, Chinese students are taking part in the fund-raising activities.

Sustainable development

The huge increase in the world's population over the past 50 years, and the rapid economic growth of previously poor nations such as India and China (above), have together put a strain on the world's natural resources, such as oil, gas and water. Environmentalists, aid workers and economists are now looking at ways in which economic development can sustain rather than exploit these resources for the benefit of future generations.

Alternative energy sources

It has become clear that humans are having a harmful impact on the world's climate. Pollution from cars, aeroplanes and industry has contributed to a steady rise in temperatures. This may result in the melting of ice caps and glaciers, causing sea levels to rise and flood many low-lying parts of the world. 'Renewable' forms of energy, such as wind power (below), are increasingly being used, because they do not produce any of the 'greenhouse gases' that contribute to global warming.

Vast rows of wind turbines are now a common sight in isolated or mountainous locations such as the Tehachapi Pass in California, USA. Wind farms have been generating electricity in this region since the early 1980s.

Index

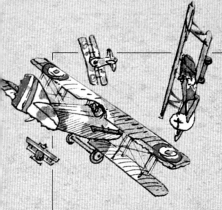

This index lists the main peoples, places and topics that you will find in the text in this book. It is not a full index of all the place names and physical features to be found on the maps.

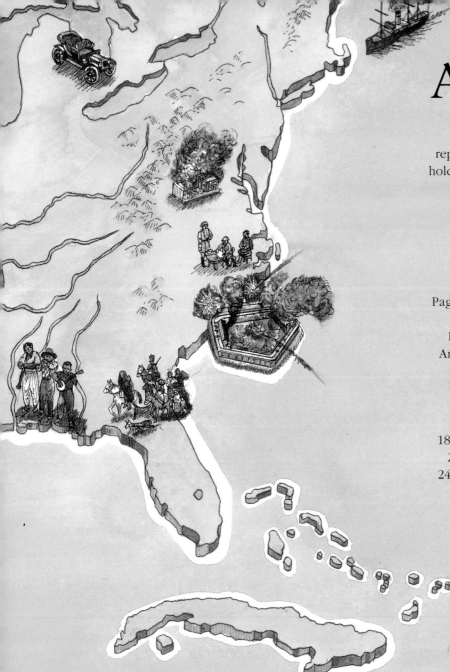

Acknowledgements

The publisher would like to thank the following for permission to reproduce their material. Every care has been taken to trace copyright holders. However, if there have been unintentional omissions or failure to trace copyright holders, we apologize and will, if informed, endeavour to make corrections in any future edition.

Key: *b* = bottom, *c* = centre, *l* = left, *r* = right, *t* = top

Pages 6*tl* and 6*c* Corbis/Bettmann; 6*b* Corbis/epa; 7*l* Corbis/Ron Watts; 7*r* Alamy/Jan Tadeusz; 7*ctr* Alamy/Tetra Images; 7*cbr* Alamy/David Hancock; 8 Art Archive/Musée du Louvre/Dagli Orti; 10*t* Bridgeman Art Library/Dallas Historical Society; 10*b* Bridgeman Art Library/Leeds Museums & Art Galleries; 11*tl* Getty/Hulton Archive; 11*c* Heritage Image Partnership/Topfoto/Ann Ronan; 11*b* Getty/George Eastman House; 12 Bridgeman Art Library/V&A Museum; 14 Bridgeman Art Library/Medford Historical Society Collection; 17 Corbis/Bettmann; 18 Bridgeman Art Library/Musée de la ville de Paris/Archive Charmet; 21 Corbis; 22 Corbis/Sygma/Thomas Johnson; 24*tl* Corbis/Bettmann; 24*bl* Getty/Savill; 24*br* Corbis/Sunset Boulevard; 25*t* Corbis/Bettmann; 25*b* Corbis/Underwood & Underwood; 26 Corbis/Hulton-Deutsch Collection; 28 Corbis; 31 Getty/Tom Stoddart; 32 Getty/AFP; 34 Corbis/Swim Ink 2; 37 Art Archive/Musée du Chateau de Versailles; 38 Art Archive/The Travel Site; 41 Getty/Keystone; 43 Getty Gerard Cerles; 44*tr* Corbis/Gideon Mendel; 44*b* Getty Toyohiro Yamada; 45*tl* Getty Per-Anders Pettersson; 45*cl* Getty Images; 45*cr* Corbis/Reuters/ Nir Elias; 45*b* Getty/National Geographic Society/Marc Moritsch.

The publisher would like to thank the following illustrators: *Cover* and page 1 Mark Bergin; additional illustrations on pages 16, 17, 18, 19, 32 and 33 also by Mark Bergin. All other illustrations by Kevin Maddison.